Stress Management

About the series

Your Personal Trainer is a series of five books designed to help you learn, or develop, key business skills. Fun, flexible and involving (and written by experienced, real-life trainers), each title in the series acts as your very own 'personal fitness trainer', allowing you to focus on your own individual experience and identify priorities for action.

Assertiveness	1 904298 13 3
Stress Management	1 904298 17 6
Interviewing Skills	1 904298 14 1
Negotiating Skills	1 904298 15 X
Time Management	1 904298 16 8

Stress Management

by Jeanie Civil

First published in 2003 by
Spiro Press
17-19 Rochester Row
London SW1P 1LA
Telephone: +44 (0)870 400 1000

© Jeanie Civil, 2003

© Typographical arrangement, Spiro Press, 2003

ISBN 1 904298 17 6

British Library Cataloguing-in-Publication Data.
A catalogue record for this book is available from the British Library.

Library of Congress Cataloging-in-Publication. Data on file.

All rights reserved. No part of this publication may be reproduced, stored in a retrieval system or transmitted, in any form or by any means, electronic, mechanical, photocopying, recording and/or otherwise without the prior written permission of the publishers. This book may not be lent, resold, hired out or otherwise disposed of by way of trade in any form, binding or cover other than that in which it is published without the prior written permission of the publishers.

Jeanie Civil asserts her moral right to be identified as the author of this work.

Series devised by: Astrid French and Susannah Lear
Series Editor: Astrid French

Spiro Press USA
3 Front Street
Suite 331
PO Box 338
Rollinsford NH 03869
USA

Typeset by: Wyvern 21 Ltd, Bristol
Printed in Great Britain by: Cromwell Press
Cover image by: Gettyimages
Cover design by: Cachet Creatives

Dedicated to Brenda Mallon, my dearest pal

Contents

Introduction ix

How to use this book xiii

Fitness Assessment 1
Test your current skills fitness

Are you stressed? 5
1 Physical signs 5
2 Psychological signs 6
3 Behavioural signs 7

Sources of stress 9
4 Work or home stress? 9
5 Time and workload management 16
6 Communication 19
7 Dealing with people 21
8 Dealing with conflict 24

About you 28
9 Thinking, feeling and behaving 29
10 Assertiveness 31

Fitness Profile 35
Strengths and weaknesses identified

Are you stressed? 39
1 Physical signs 39
2 Psychological signs 39
3 Behavioural signs 40

Sources of stress 42
4 Work or home stress? 43
5 Time and workload management 44

6 Communication	45
7 Dealing with people	46
8 Dealing with conflict	49
About you	55
9 Thinking, feeling and behaving	55
10 Assertiveness	58

How good are you at stress management? 61

Warm-up 63

Work-out 65
Activities and exercises to build your fitness

Are you stressed?	69
1 Physical signs	69
2 Psychological signs	70
3 Behavioural signs	74
Sources of stress	77
4 Work or home stress?	77
5 Time and workload management	79
6 Communication	83
7 Dealing with people	85
8 Dealing with conflict	87
About you	91
9 Thinking, feeling and behaving	91
10 Assertiveness	93

Keeping Fit 99

Further Reading/Bibliography 105

Introduction

Welcome to *Stress Management*, part of a series – **Your Personal Trainer** – that offers you an exciting new way to learn, or develop, key business skills. Fun, flexible and involving, each title in this series acts as your very own 'personal fitness trainer', allowing you to focus on your individual experience and identify priorities for action.

Designed as a self-development workbook, each title creates an individual record of what you have achieved.

This book focuses on developing your *stress management* skills, a key skill for success and happiness at both work and home. It gives you the opportunity to assess where you are now, and opens doors for where you might like to go, or be, in the future.

> *WATCH OUT FOR YOUR TRAINER*
> *He will give you tips and alert you to potential problems as you work your way through the book.*

Everyone is capable of managing their stress, though there will be challenges to meet along the way. Becoming 'fit' in stress management is as much about confidence, self-esteem and thinking patterns as it is about techniques. The ideas and exercises in this book may be a little uncomfortable at first. However, by keeping an open mind and putting in some practice, managing your stress will become part of your everyday responses.

To be described as stress free may not always feel like a compliment! This could be because so many people confuse this state with being laid back and uninvolved. Hence, 'She just doesn't seem to care' or 'He isn't at all concerned with what's going on.' Not so! If you are able to manage your pressures and minimize your stress, then these comments are invalid. What, then, is stress?

What is stress?

First, we need to recognize that not all stress is bad. A certain amount of stress (or pressure if you prefer) can inspire and improve performance, but too much (or when the demands of life seem too great to cope with and/or we feel we lack support) and it becomes a problem.

The ability to handle pressure varies from person to person, and what one person finds stressful may not be a problem for another. We also suffer different symptoms of stress. How you respond to stress depends on how you think and feel, how you view the world (your 'filters'); becoming aware of this will help you to manage your stress.

What is stress management?

Of course, there are difficult life events that will cause sadness, grief and pressure – the most potentially stressful being bereavement, not just death but also the loss of a partner, job, money, home, children and status. However, there are positive and negative ways of coping with these and other events. Stress management is about identifying, and then positively managing, your sources of stress.

So what do you gain, or lose, by managing your stress?

You gain:
- ✓ a sense of humour
- ✓ enjoyment
- ✓ friends
- ✓ a harmonious life
- ✓ the avoidance of conflict
- ✓ acceptance of your inner feelings
- ✓ a healthy body.

You lose:
- ✗ the ability to rush about
- ✗ the comfort of knowing you are unable to clear the atmosphere of conflict

- ✗ the sympathy of others
- ✗ the comfort of not being able to make decisions
- ✗ the comfort of knowing you always fail in relationships
- ✗ psychosomatic illness.

And what do you gain, or lose, by failing to manage your stress?

You gain:
- ✓ nothing.

You lose:
- ✗ your sense of humour
- ✗ self-love and self-worth
- ✗ self-confidence
- ✗ quality of life
- ✗ trust
- ✗ respect
- ✗ influence
- ✗ genuine relationships.

So, ask yourself the question; are you happy with your gains, or are the losses in your life greater? Would you give up some of the gains of not managing your stress for the positive aspects of being mentally happier and healthier?

If so, read on…

This is a book for anyone who wants to learn the physical, psychological and behavioural skills of managing stress, and have some fun while doing so! Whether developing your stress management skills from scratch, or brushing up on what you already know, enjoy your read, and enjoy the benefits of managing your stress.

How to use this book

This book has been produced in a flexible format so you can maximize your individual potential for learning. You will have to put some work into it, but you should have some fun along the way!

The book is divided into four main parts:
Fitness Assessment
Fitness Profile
Work-out
Keeping Fit.

Fitness Assessment consists of 10 individual assessments. These assessments are grouped into three key skills areas or *sections*:

Are you stressed?
Sources of stress, and
About you.

The assessments offer a range of questions, exercises, choices of behaviour and attitudes to test your current stress management 'fitness'.

Try and be as honest and objective as possible when completing this part so that you have a realistic idea of your current skills fitness. And remember, there are no right or wrong answers, only feedback!

Fitness Profile gives you the results of your Fitness Assessment. It helps you to understand your responses and identify both personal strengths and weaknesses/areas for development.

Work-out offers a range of practical activities and exercises to improve your skills and help you become 'super-fit' at stress management!

Keeping Fit reminds you of the importance of practising your skills and allows you to develop a personal fitness plan.

You will get the most out of this book if you work through it systematically, checking up on your stress management skills from 1-10. This will enable you to get a good overall view of your fitness.

However, you may choose to focus on a particular area of the skill (eg identifying your sources of stress), working through the relevant section in Fitness Assessment then moving on to subsequent sections in Fitness Profile and Work-out. These sections are clearly identified in the text, with directions to follow-up reading marked with an arrow *at the end of each section*.

Finally, if you want a quick review of key learning points, check out the summary checklists at the end of each section in Work-out.

Whichever way you choose to use this book, enjoy the experience!

Fitness Assessment

Fitness Assessment

Fitness Assessment has been designed to test your current skills fitness.

If you want an overall picture of your skills fitness (which is recommended), you need to work through all 10 assessments and then move on to subsequent parts – Fitness Profile, Work-out and Keeping Fit.

*However, if you don't have the time to work through all 10 assessments, or wish to focus your learning, you can concentrate on those sections which develop a particular aspect of the skill, and then only work through relevant subsequent sections. If you do decide to do this, however, make sure that you work through **all** the assessments within the individual sections.*

Assessments 1-3 *focus on* **Are you stressed?**
Assessments 4-8 *on* **Sources of stress**
Assessments 9-10 *focus on* **About you**.

So, let's test your current skills fitness.

Are you stressed?

> **TRAINER'S WARNING**
> Don't forget to answer these questions honestly; make sure you get a true picture of your fitness.

Stress can affect you physically, psychologically and behaviourally. Different people will be affected differently and will have different responses to stress. The following three assessments focus on identifying potential signs or symptoms of stress.

> **TRAINER'S TIP**
> Feel free to change the genders in any of the examples offered; you may find this helps you to relate better to the situations.

ASSESSMENT 1: PHYSICAL SIGNS

> **TRAINER'S WARNING**
> Serious or prolonged physical symptoms need to be checked out by a doctor.

Even though you may think that you are coping, if you really are feeling up against it, then stress will eventually emerge. Often, it manifests itself in physical signs or symptoms. Watch out for these physical symptoms of stress; take heed of your body's messages and warnings.

What is your 'Achilles' heel'? In other words, which part of your body is a warning light to you that you are stressed? Below are some common physical symptoms of stress. Which do you experience? (Tick as many as apply.)

1. Muscle tension or pain ☐
2. Nail biting ☐
3. Lack of appetite ☐
4. Bowel abnormalities ☐
5. Dry mouth ☐
6. Fatigue/tiredness/exhaustion ☐
7. Headaches/migraine ☐

8 Sexual dysfunctions	☐
9 Insomnia	☐
10 Sweating	☐
11 Restlessness	☐
12 Tingling in body	☐
13 Feeling bloated	☐
14 Breathlessness or palpitations	☐
15 Nausea	☐
16 Lack of co-ordination/clumsiness	☐
17 Anxiety in stomach/cramps	☐
18 Foot or leg aches	☐
19 Increased breathing rate	☐
20 Twitching of hands/legs/face	☐
21 Shaking	☐
22 Red skin blotches, flushes	☐

Number of boxes ticked   SCORE

ASSESSMENT 2: PSYCHOLOGICAL SIGNS

TRAINER'S WARNING

Serious or prolonged psychological symptoms need to be checked out by a doctor.

As with physical symptoms, sometimes there may be justifiable reasons for experiencing certain psychological emotions or thought processes. However, as with physical symptoms, they also may be indicators that you are experiencing more than a motivating amount of pressure.

What are your psychological signs? Which of the following do you experience? (Tick as many as apply.)

1 Blocking off positive emotions or experiences ☐
2 A downward spiral of feelings ☐
3 Lack of concentration ☐
4 Anger/aggression ☐
5 Anxiety/anxiety-inducing dreams ☐
6 Confusion ☐

7 Feelings of being unable to cope ☐
8 Frequently wanting to cry ☐
9 Wishing to escape or run away ☐
10 Indecisiveness/apathy ☐
11 Defensiveness ☐
12 Sexual disinterest ☐
13 Lack of self-love ☐
14 Low self-esteem ☐
15 Depression ☐
16 Feeling highly emotional; mood swings ☐
17 Lack of self-control ☐
18 Panic ☐
19 Paranoia ☐
20 Feelings of isolation ☐
21 Feelings of being betrayed or rejected ☐
22 Feelings of jealousy or envy ☐

Number of boxes ticked   SCORE

What is your most likely psychological symptom, when you feel that you are under pressure? ....
....

ASSESSMENT 3: BEHAVIOURAL SIGNS

How you respond to pressure affects your behaviour. If you feel stressed out by people or events, this will often be reflected in your behaviour.

1 Behavioural signs

Below is a list of common behavioural signs or symptoms. Which of them do you experience? (Tick as many as apply.)

A Wanting to stay in more than usual ☐
B Overeating ☐

C Going without food ☐
D Increased drinking ☐
E Increased smoking ☐
F Irritability with family and friends ☐
G Awaking early ☐
H Fidgeting, tapping of feet ☐
I An inability to manage time effectively ☐
J Temper outbursts ☐

Number of boxes ticked SCORE

2 Speech

Look at the following examples of stressful speech. How many do you use? Ask someone you trust whether they have noticed you using such speech. Tick as many boxes as apply.

A Speaking unintelligibly ☐
B Speaking too loudly or too quietly ☐
C Putting yourself down ☐
D Being overly apologetic ☐
E Finishing off people's sentences ☐
F Talking 'over' somebody ☐

Number of boxes ticked SCORE

3 Body language

Your body talks! How you think and feel about yourself, situations and people is reflected in your body language. This in turn is picked up and interpreted by those around you. Body language may be interpreted as:

Avoiding (withdrawn, retiring)
Adapting (compromising)
Appeasing (pleasing others)
Aggressive (threatening)
Assertive (direct, open)

Listed below are some common examples of body language. What might this body language be 'saying'? Do you use such body language regularly? Again, ask someone you trust to advise you, then tick as many boxes as apply.

A   Little or no eye contact   ☐
B   Shaking hands too hard, or too loose   ☐
C   Pointing finger   ☐
D   Twirling hair   ☐
E   Hands on mouth   ☐
F   Smiling too much   ☐

Number of boxes ticked   SCORE

Ideally, you should work through all 10 assessments to get an overall view of your stress management 'fitness'. If, however, you wish to focus on whether, and how much, you are stressed ➡ Are you stressed? Fitness Profile p.39.

Sources of stress

TRAINER'S WARNING
Answer these questions honestly; make sure you get a true picture of your fitness.

Potentially, anything could be a source or cause of stress (a 'stressor'), it's how you respond that counts. Stress can come from your work or home life, from particular situations or people.

In order to manage stress, you first need to identify its cause. Assessments 4-8 focus on identifying your individual causes of stress.

TRAINER'S TIP
Feel free to change the genders or personnel in any of the examples offered; you may find this helps you relate to the situations.

ASSESSMENT 4: WORK OR HOME STRESS?

You can become stressed out by people and events at both

work and home. Sometimes you can feel stressed in one environment and not the other; or sometimes both can be stressing you out. Where do you feel stressed?

1 Day-to-day stresses at work

Below is a list of statements that reflect common, day-to-day sources of stress at work. How many do you recognize? How often do you think or feel this way? Circle either 0, 1, 2, 3 or 4 as described in the key below.

KEY

- **0** I always think or feel this
- **1** I often think or feel this
- **2** I sometimes think or feel this
- **3** I rarely think or feel this
- **4** I never think or feel this

A	I am unclear about what is expected of me.	0 1 2 3 4
B	My co-workers seem unclear about what my job is.	0 1 2 3 4
C	I have differences of opinion with my superiors.	0 1 2 3 4
D	I feel I always have to put work above family commitments.	0 1 2 3 4
E	I lack confidence in management.	0 1 2 3 4
F	Management expects me to interrupt my work for new priorities.	0 1 2 3 4
G	Conflict exists between my section/department and others it must work with.	0 1 2 3 4
H	I get feedback only when my performance is unsatisfactory.	0 1 2 3 4
I	Decisions or changes that affect me are made without my knowledge or involvement.	0 1 2 3 4
J	I must attend meetings to get my job done.	0 1 2 3 4
K	I am cautious about what I say in meetings.	0 1 2 3 4

L	I don't feel I am listened to.	0 1 2 3 4
M	I feel over-managed.	0 1 2 3 4
N	I feel under-managed.	0 1 2 3 4
O	I feel over-qualified for the work I actually do.	0 1 2 3 4
P	I feel under-qualified for the work I actually do.	0 1 2 3 4
Q	The people I work with closely are trained in a field that is different from mine.	0 1 2 3 4
R	I must go to other departments to get my job done.	0 1 2 3 4
S	I have unsettled conflicts with my co-workers.	0 1 2 3 4
T	I get no personal support from my co-workers.	0 1 2 3 4
U	I do not have the right amount of interaction (too much or too little) with others.	0 1 2 3 4
V	I spend my time 'fighting fires' rather than working according to plan.	0 1 2 3 4

Now add up your scores　　　　　　　　　SCORE

2 Work 'events'

Listed below are some common work 'events' that may cause stress. The 'score' of each event reflects the degree of disruption it causes in the average person's life (that is, it represents the average amount, severity or duration of personal adjustment required to restore equilibrium after experiencing the event).

Generally, the lower the score the greater the probability of stress and potential health problems in the near future (Holmes and Rabe, 1967). However, since individuals vary in their tolerance for stress, the total score should be taken as a rough guide only.

Look at the following list. How many of these work events have you experienced in the past 12 months? Put a tick in the appropriate box/boxes, next to the average [value] 'score'. The events are 'ranked', with the potentially most stressful at number 1.

Rank	Event	Value/Score	
1	Being transferred against my will to a new position or assignment.	−20	☐
2	Being shelved (moved to a less important job).	−19	☐
3	Experiencing a decrease in status (either actual or in relation to my peers).	−17	☐
4	Being disciplined or seriously reprimanded by my supervisor.	−17	☐
5	Having my request to transfer to a new, more satisfying, job rejected.	−15	☐
6	Sustaining a sudden, significant change in the nature of my work.	−15	☐
7	Learning of the cancellation of a project I was involved with and considered important.	−15	☐
8	Encountering major or frequent changes in instructions, policies or procedures.	−15	☐
9	Being promoted or advanced at a slower rate than I expected.	−14	☐
10	Being transferred voluntarily to a new position or assignment (not a promotion).	−13	☐
11	Anticipating my own imminent retirement.	−12	☐
12	Undergoing a major reorganization (at least throughout my department).	−11	☐
13	Experiencing a sudden decrease in the number of positive recognitions of my accomplishments (from any source).	−11	☐
14	Encountering a major change (increase or decrease) in the		

	technology affecting my job (computers, techniques etc).	−11	☐
15	Giving a major briefing or formal presentation.	−11	☐
16	Acquiring a new boss or supervisor.	−11	☐
17	Sustaining a sudden, significant decrease in the activity level or pace of my work.	−10	☐
18	Sustaining a sudden, significant increase in the activity level or pace of my work.	−9	☐
19	Undergoing a major relocation of my workplace.	−8	☐
20	Experiencing an increase in status (either actual or in relation to my peers).	−8	☐
21	Being required to work more hours per week than normal due to crises or deadlines.	−7	☐
22	Experiencing the transfer, resignation, termination or retirement of a close friend or valued colleague.	−6	☐
23	Being promoted or advanced at a faster rate than I expected.	−6	☐
24	Acquiring new subordinates.	−6	☐
25	Acquiring new co-workers.	−5	☐
26	Experiencing an increase in the number of positive recognitions of my accomplishments (from any source).	−4	☐

Now add together your scores   SCORE

List below, in order, the item ('rank') numbers of the three events you personally felt to be the most stressful:

1 ....
2 ....
3 ....

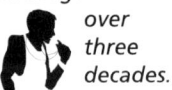

3 Life 'events'

Some people seem to sail through life, while others appear to have to cope with so many heartaches and happenings. These life events are valued on a guidance scale, which corresponds to the possible effect they may have on your stress levels and health. They have also been 'ranked', with the potentially most stressful at number 1.

Look through the following list. How many of these life events have you experienced during the last year? Put a tick in the appropriate box/boxes, next to the average [value] 'score'.

> **TRAINER'S WARNING**
>
> *This is only one indicator of possible stress adapted by Jeanie Civil from the Holmes-Rabe scale of stress ratings and from her experience in training in stress management for over three decades.*

Rank	Event	Value/Score	
1	Bereavement – death of wife, husband, partner, child, close friend	–25	☐
2	Divorce	–19	☐
3	Sexual difficulties	–16	☐
4	Moving house	–16	☐
5	Marital separation	–16	☐
6	Imprisonment	–15	☐
7	Personal injury or illness	–12	☐
8	Marriage	–12	☐
9	Made redundant	–12	☐
10	Marital reconciliation	–12	☐
11	Death of a loved pet	–12	☐
12	Retirement	–12	☐
13	Change in health of family member	–10	☐

14	Pregnancy	−10	☐
15	Loss or gain of a family member	−10	☐
16	Business readjustment	−10	☐
17	Change in financial state	−9	☐
18	Change to different line of work (new responsibilities)	−9	☐
19	Change in number of arguments with spouse	−9	☐
20	Large mortgage	−8	☐
21	Foreclosure of mortgage or loan	−8	☐
22	Setting up a new partnership in home sharing	−8	☐
23	Son or daughter leaving or returning home	−8	☐
24	House extensions/significant building project	−8	☐
25	Trouble with in-laws	−8	☐
26	Outstanding personal achievement	−8	☐
27	Partner begins or stops work	−6	☐
28	Beginning or ending a period of study	−6	☐
29	Trouble with line manager	−6	☐
30	Christmas recently (within last two months)	−6	☐
31	Change in working hours or conditions of service	−5	☐
32	Change in recreation	−5	☐
33	Change in religious or cultural activities	−5	☐
34	Change in social activities	−4	☐
35	Large personal loan	−4	☐
36	Change in sleeping habits	−4	☐
37	Change in number of family get-togethers	−4	☐
38	Change in eating habits	−4	☐

| 39 | Vacation recently | –4 | ☐ |
| 40 | Minor violations of the law recently (motor offences etc) | –3 | ☐ |

Now add together your scores   SCORE

ASSESSMENT 5: TIME AND WORKLOAD MANAGEMENT

Your attitude to your work, and how well you organize it, affects how stressful you find the work situation.

1 Are you a 'workaholic'?

Look at the following statements. How well do they describe your behaviour? Circle either 0, 1, 2 or 3 as shown in the following key.

KEY
0 I often do or think this
1 I sometimes do or think this
2 I rarely do or think this
3 I never do or think this

A	I talk about my work in social settings.	0 1 2 3
B	I find it easier to talk about my work than about most other things.	0 1 2 3
C	I often feel stressed by my job.	0 1 2 3
D	I take on excessive workloads.	0 1 2 3
E	I resent having to take holidays.	0 1 2 3
F	I work during the weekend.	0 1 2 3
G	I take work home in the evenings.	0 1 2 3
H	I am energetic and competitive.	0 1 2 3
I	I eat lunch alone.	0 1 2 3
J	I work while I am eating.	0 1 2 3
K	I find it difficult to do nothing.	0 1 2 3
L	I can work anywhere, anytime.	0 1 2 3
M	I allow insufficient time for play.	0 1 2 3

N I pay insufficient attention to health. 0 1 2 3

Now add up your scores   SCORE

2 Do you have a time management problem?

Again, look at the following statements. How well do they describe your feelings and behaviour? Circle either 0, 1, 2 or 3 as described in the key below. Work quickly; first impressions are usually quite accurate.

KEY
- **0** I quite often do, think or feel this
- **1** I sometimes do, think or feel this
- **2** I rarely do, think or feel this
- **3** I never do, think or feel this

A	I can't get on with my work because of interruptions.	0 1 2 3
B	Problems that I have not forseen interfere with my work.	0 1 2 3
C	Most of my time is under my own control.	0 1 2 3
D	I have too much to do and too little time in which to do it.	0 1 2 3
E	I don't have enough to do.	0 1 2 3
F	I feel I have a good balance between my work and home life.	0 1 2 3
G	Colleagues take my time without making an adequate contribution to my effectiveness.	0 1 2 3
H	I feel I'm always letting down my kids, missing birthday parties and school plays.	0 1 2 3
I	Poorly design systems in the organization waste my time.	0 1 2 3
J	I find tasks to keep me busy, avoiding things I should be doing.	0 1 2 3

K	I keep my work in piles on my desk, on shelves, by the phone etc.	0 1 2 3
L	Delegation is a waste of time, I can do things better and quicker myself.	0 1 2 3
M	I put off difficult or big jobs.	0 1 2 3
N	My door is always open; colleagues can speak to me at any time.	0 1 2 3
O	Meetings take up too much of my time.	0 1 2 3
P	Decisions and actions are followed up in a timely and effective way.	0 1 2 3
Q	I waste time looking for files, papers etc.	0 1 2 3
R	Some of my work could be delegated to more junior colleagues.	0 1 2 3
S	Procrastination keeps me from completing work on time.	0 1 2 3
T	I work longer hours than I am required to do.	0 1 2 3
U	I set priorities for each piece of work I have to do.	0 1 2 3
V	I organize my work in the office systematically.	0 1 2 3
W	I list tasks on a 'to do' list to keep my priorities before me.	0 1 2 3
X	I ask myself 'Am I working on the right thing, in the right way, right now?'	0 1 2 3

Now you need to work out your scores. For this assessment there are two scores. First, add up your scores for questions A, B, D, E, G, H I, J, K, L, M, N, O, Q, S and T.

This is your **'A' score** SCORE

Now add up your scores for the remaining questions; this is your **'B' score** SCORE

ASSESSMENT 6: COMMUNICATION

'Why do I find it easy to communicate with some people and not others?'

Some people simply are difficult to communicate with – maybe they keep interrupting, maybe they don't listen or try to manipulate you. This can cause confusion, frustration – and stress. However, your ability to communicate with people can also be affected by something fundamental to you – the thoughts, feelings and attitudes you hold towards them. How do you feel about the people you work with, whether they are people you manage or who manage you? And how do these feelings affect your ability to communicate?

Generally, you communicate better with people you like. People you like usually share your values (on politics, religion, race, gender and sexuality). You find it easier to communicate with them as you are starting from the same point of view and already 'speak the same language'. Conversely, you tend to communicate less well with people you dislike. Sometimes you dislike people with good reason – maybe they have broken your trust; maybe they hold sexist or racist views. Beware, however, of not liking people for the wrong reasons – maybe they got a job you applied for; maybe they simply have the wrong accent or you don't like their dress sense. Maybe they remind you of someone you dislike, or maybe they remind you of something about yourself you don't like (projection).

1 Communicating with colleagues

TRAINER'S WARNING

Answer these questions as honestly as you can. There are no right or wrong answers.

In the space overleaf, list six colleagues with whom you have good two-way communication and work well; this is your 'A' list. If you can't name six, then list as many as you can.

'A' list

....
....
....
....
....
....

Now list six colleagues with whom you have poor communication and don't work well; this is your 'B' list. Again, if you can't name six people list as many as you can.

'B' list

....
....
....
....
....
....

2 Likes and dislikes

Look at the following questions and fill in the blanks.

A Who do you like at work? ....
(If you are resistant to the word 'like' change it to 'get on with', 'enjoy working with' or 'find easy to work with')

B Who do you dislike at work? ....
(Again, if you are querying the word 'dislike', change it into your own preferred language)

C Who do you trust at work, ie who do you believe will not abuse you to others or relay confidential disclosures?
....

D Who have you trusted in the past and now find that this trust has been broken or betrayed? ....
....

(If you can't think of someone at work, what about outside work?)

E Who do you think has been promoted beyond their ability (even though they may have the 'qualifications')?

....

F Who intellectually stimulates you? ....

....

(Think of someone against whom you can pit your wits, or with whom you enjoy stimulating banter)

G Who has a good sense of humour and makes you laugh?

....

H To whom are you sexually attracted? ....

....

I Towards whom do you have positive/friendly feelings?

....

J Towards whom do you have negative or unfriendly feelings?...

ASSESSMENT 7: DEALING WITH PEOPLE

Whether at work or home, how other people behave, and how you respond, will affect you, and your stress levels.

1 Saying No to a particular person

Saying No to a particular person (whether to a specific request or simply disagreeing with them) can be difficult, even for naturally assertive people. Perhaps you feel intimidated by the other person, or they remind you of someone you used to be afraid of. Perhaps you are seeking their approval or resent their success. Perhaps your family values and culture encourage you to defer to authority figures. Whatever the reason, if you fail to say No to people you can end up feeling overloaded and put upon; you can feel stressed.

Look at the following list of people. To whom do you find it difficult to say No? Tick the relevant box/boxes.

A	A life partner	☐
B	One of your children	☐
C	A certain relative	☐
D	One of your friends	☐
E	A business partner	☐
F	An employer/your boss	☐
G	A colleague	☐
H	A specific teacher	☐
I	A doctor	☐
J	A police officer	☐
K	A lawyer	☐
L	Other people	☐

Name them..

How many boxes did you tick? Make a note of the number here   SCORE

2 Dealing with manipulation

Being manipulated, whether consciously or not, can be stressful. When people try to manipulate you they are looking for some kind of pay-off; this means they gain something for themselves, either a certain feeling or something specific they want from you. You need to be able to recognize what manipulators are trying to achieve for themselves, otherwise it prevents you from achieving your goals, which leads to stress.

Generally, people will try to manipulate you by working on certain 'psychological triggers' or perceived weaknesses. They may try to:

A Work on your vulnerabilities or 'crumple button'
B Appeal to your emotions
C Appeal to your intellect

- D   Hook your childhood messages
- E   Play on your friendship
- F   Use their status
- G   Appeal to your values
- H   Play on your loyalty
- I   Make you look foolish or put you down
- J   Get what they want, regardless of your needs.

Manipulators often tell you their needs when you are asking for what you need, justify their position and simply refuse to listen.

Try to identify what kind of manipulation is being used in the following examples. Choose the appropriate letter from A-J and write it in the box provided.

1 'I realize that you're keen to get away for the weekend, but could you just do this photocopying for me before you leave?' ☐

2 'You are the best public speaker we have, so I want you, rather than me, to give this presentation to the staff.' ☐

3 'I recognize that you have to go to a funeral, however, you must be back by 4pm for this important meeting.' ☐

4 'I know how loyal you are to me as your boss, so you have to attend the residential conference regardless of the difficulties you are having with your partner.' ☐

5 'I understand how disappointed you were when you didn't get the last promotion, but this will give you the opportunity to show how the wrong person was promoted.' ☐

6 'I expect you to refer all ideas and queries to me as your line manager before mentioning them to the directors.' ☐

ASSESSMENT 8: DEALING WITH CONFLICT

Conflict, in one form or another, is an inevitable part of working life. It can range from muted disagreement through raised voices, sometimes even violence. It can occur between team members or between managers and staff; it can even involve external clients or suppliers. Whatever its form or vehemence, if not handled appropriately, conflict can be a major cause of stress. What is your current attitude towards conflict; how do you currently deal with conflict?

1 Your attitude to conflict

Check out the following situation. How would you respond? (Tick the appropriate box.)

Your client complains to you about your overly bureaucratic system. What do you do?

A Agree with them about the stupid rules. ☐
B Tell them that they deserve to be delayed and that it's their fault. ☐
C Ask them to tell you the facts of the case and then act on the evidence presented. ☐
D Say 'It's nothing to do with me.' ☐
E Say 'Don't worry, it will turn out all right.' ☐

2 Identifying and managing conflict

Before you can manage conflict, you first need to be able to recognize and identify it.

Conflict can take a number of different forms:
Inner conflict (when what you have to do is different from what you want to do)
Organizational conflict (when the organizational culture and values are different from your own)
Team conflict
Conflict between two people for whom you have responsibility, and
Conflict with one other person.

Read through the following scenarios. What form of conflict do they involve? Now tick your most likely response to these scenarios.

1. You are experiencing personal, family or relationship problems; you need to take some time off work. How do you respond?
   A Say nothing. ☐
   B Talk with someone you like to gain reassurance that it is not your fault. ☐
   C Tell half-truths: consider taking sick leave.
   D Stay at work and involve yourself in frantic activity. ☐
   E Discuss with your line manager that you are having some personal difficulties and that it may be necessary to have some time away from work, which you will make up. ☐

2. You are receiving complaints from several members of your staff about the slackness of one of the team. What do you do or say?
   A Say nothing. ☐
   B Smile at the team member concerned when you see them. ☐
   C Suggest that the rest of the team do a little extra work to cover. ☐
   D See the person concerned and tell them to perform to standard, otherwise face the disciplinary procedure. ☐
   E Call the team together and ask them to voice their concerns about the 'team dynamics' or responsibilities. ☐

3. You have to make five redundancies. How do you respond?
   A Do nothing; things might change. ☐
   B Worry about each person; consider their home life and how they will suffer. ☐

C Decide which five you want to go, based upon your redundancy policy, but don't take any action. ☐
D Talk to all staff about the redundancies. Ask for volunteers first, and then draw up a 'possibles' list, following consultation with staff and in the light of company regulations. ☐
E Suggest to your line manager that you could make some people part-time. ☐

4 Two of your staff have conflict between them. They each come separately to you and complain about the other. How do you deal with the problem?
  A Bring the two of them together and ask them to tell each other what the issues are, and how they can be resolved. ☐
  B Agree with each person that it must be difficult. Say that you are glad that they feel they can come and talk to you, but do nothing. ☐
  C Suggest that they do the jobs they think they can manage to do without much difficulty and forget the area of conflict. ☐
  D Say that you are not there to sort out relationships; you have more important targets to achieve. ☐
  E Take no notice. ☐

5 You are experiencing unjust treatment, bullying or harassment from someone at work. How do you respond?
  A Avoid the person. ☐
  B Talk to the person concerned about the behaviour that you have observed, tell them how you feel and say what you need, in terms of their treatment of you. ☐
  C Think 'Well, they can be all right some of the time so that should be enough.' ☐
  D Tell their line manager and suggest that the person concerned should leave. ☐

E   Try to be nice to them. Exchange pleasantries each time you see them.   ☐

3 Giving and receiving criticism

Practically everyone is criticized from time to time – sometimes with good reason, sometimes not; sometimes constructively, sometimes not. Receiving criticism, even justified, constructive criticism can be a stressful experience. So too giving criticism; get it wrong and you can make a situation worse.

Look at the following four situations. How would you respond? Circle either 1, 2 or 3 as described in the key below.

KEY

1 I am least likely to respond in this way
2 I might respond in this way; the other two options don't appeal
3 I am most likely to respond in this way

1 For the first time in months you are late for a one-to-one meeting. Your colleague exclaims 'You are always late for my meetings!' How do you respond?

A Walk away and get angry.	1 2 3
B Justify your behaviour.	1 2 3
C Ask for specific examples.	1 2 3

2 You are being reprimanded in front of your colleagues. How do you respond?

A Say 'I don't think it is appropriate to discuss this with other people present.'	1 2 3
B Cry.	1 2 3
C Blame other colleagues or circumstances.	1 2 3

3 Your manager has recently cancelled two meetings with you at short notice. You are annoyed and complain to a director. Your manager is then upset to receive feedback from a director rather than from you first; she questions your behaviour. How do you react?

A Say 'Well, you are never here.'		1 2 3
B Say 'I'm sorry, you are right. It won't happen again.'		1 2 3
C Say nothing, and then moan to your colleagues about what a rotten manager she is.		1 2 3

4 Some of your colleagues are feeling de-motivated; you need to pass on some critical feedback to your manager. What do you say?

A 'Two members of the team are feeling very de-motivated, mainly because you hardly ever praise them for the extra work they do for you in their own time.'	1 2 3
B 'Everyone in the team is de-motivated.'	1 2 3
C 'Everyone thinks that you're a useless manager.'	1 2 3

Ideally, you should work through all 10 assessments to get an overall view of your stress management fitness. If, however, you wish to focus on identifying your sources of stress ➡ Sources of stress Fitness Profile p.42.

About you

You are an individual, as such you have a unique response to stress. The following two assessments will help you understand how – and why – you respond in certain ways.

TRAINER'S WARNING

Remember to answer these questions honestly – make sure you get a true picture of your fitness.

TRAINER'S TIP

Feel free to change the genders or personnel in any of the examples offered; you may find this helps you to relate to the situations.

ASSESSMENT 9: THINKING, FEELING AND BEHAVING

Whether you are dealing with day-to-day stresses or a specific event, how you think and feel about yourself, other people and situations affects your behaviour. Sometimes your attitude is affected by your early childhood 'messages' – how you were told to think, feel or behave when you were small. These messages can stay with you long into adulthood, 'chatting' to you incessantly like little creatures sitting on your shoulder. Unless you become aware of them, these messages can seriously dent your self-confidence and encourage 'non-assertive' behaviour. Assertive behaviour is about addressing people and issues openly and directly; failing to do so can store up trouble, and stress.

> *Non-assertive behaviour means behaving in either an aggressive or appeasing manner. When someone is aggressive they are likely to be domineering, patronizing and stubborn towards others. Appeasing behaviour is about trying to please others; it's about withholding true feelings.*

Answer the following questions to discover your early childhood messages. Tick either the Yes or the No box for each question. If you are wavering then your answer is probably Yes. Commit yourself; don't leave a question unanswered.

		Yes	No
1	Are you reluctant to show your feelings?	☐	☐
2	When setting standards for yourself are they usually too high?	☐	☐
3	Do you sometimes feel 'put upon' when helping others?	☐	☐
4	Do you take on too many jobs at the same time?	☐	☐
5	Do you dislike letting go of a job, thinking 'with a bit more effort I could improve this task'?	☐	☐
6	Do you like to get things *right*?	☐	☐
7	Do you like to be liked, preferring to be popular than unpopular?	☐	☐

8 Do you find it difficult to delegate or ask for help? ☐ ☐

9 Do little things annoy you; a picture not quite straight, a disorderly desk, spelling mistakes? ☐ ☐

10 Do you tend to collect for somebody's present or organize your work's social gatherings? ☐ ☐

11 Do you become irritated when someone takes ages to come to the point? ☐ ☐

12 Do you use other people, or their work, as a yardstick for your own performance and judge yourself accordingly? ☐ ☐

13 Are you reluctant to give up a job, or even reading a book, which you are not enjoying? ☐ ☐

14 Do you go to work when you are feeling ill even though others would stay home with the same symptoms? ☐ ☐

15 Do you finish off, or add to, people's sentences in the hope that they'll get on with it? ☐ ☐

16 Do you like to be organized and keep things neat and tidy at home or work? ☐ ☐

17 Do you hate people wasting time talking about what they might do, instead of just doing it? ☐ ☐

18 Would you find it difficult to share your personal concerns with someone? ☐ ☐

19 Do you try to avoid conflict so as not to upset other people? ☐ ☐

20 Do you push yourself to achieve a better job or relationship, or to gain more qualifications? ☐ ☐

Complete the following five columns (A-E), putting your score next to the relevant question number (1 POINT for Yes, 0 POINTS for No). Calculate your score for each column.

Column	A	B	C	D	E
Questions	2 ☐	3 ☐	4 ☐	1 ☐	5 ☐
Questions	6 ☐	7 ☐	11 ☐	8 ☐	12 ☐
Questions	9 ☐	10 ☐	15 ☐	14 ☐	13 ☐
Questions	16 ☐	19 ☐	17 ☐	18 ☐	20 ☐
TOTAL SCORE	☐	☐	☐	☐	☐

ASSESSMENT 10: ASSERTIVENESS

One major source of stress is lack of assertiveness. If you lack assertiveness, you are less able to address issues, people and problems honestly and directly. You find it difficult to address conflict, to express your opinion or say No; you can end up overlooked, overworked and overstressed. Behaving assertively requires confidence. If you feel confident in yourself then your behaviour will naturally be more assertive and you will feel less stressed. If you lack confidence, however, you may behave less assertively. How confident do you feel; how assertively do you behave?

Read through the following situations; how confident do you feel in each individual situation? Circle either 1, 2 or 3 as described in the key below.

KEY
1 I feel tense and unconfident
2 I feel moderately OK
3 I feel positive and confident

1 Expressing your feelings
  A Expressing your anger directly and honestly
     when you feel angry.   1 2 3
  B Refusing to apologize as you believe that you
     are right, even though others expect you to
     do so.   1 2 3
  C Requesting the return of a borrowed item like
     money or a book without being apologetic.   1 2 3

D Telling someone that you feel upset about how they have treated you. 1 2 3

2 Giving and receiving compliments
A Receiving a compliment by saying something assertive to acknowledge that you agree with the person complimenting you. 1 2 3
B Getting the approval of someone significant in your life. 1 2 3
C Telling someone that they have done something well. 1 2 3
D Being told that you are a wonderful partner, parent, sibling, colleague, manager or friend. 1 2 3

3 Speaking in meetings
A Giving your opinion at a meeting. 1 2 3
B Saying you don't understand something. 1 2 3
C Asking someone to keep to the point. 1 2 3
D Asking someone to stop interrupting. 1 2 3

4 Saying No to a particular request
A When your boss asks you to work late, and you already have an engagement. 1 2 3
B When you are asked to help in a voluntary capacity for charity. 1 2 3
C When you are asked to give a colleague a lift, even though it's out of your way. 1 2 3
D When someone requests a financial loan from you. 1 2 3

5 Establishing your values
A Commenting about a racist remark made in a group. 1 2 3
B Addressing a patronizing put-down about your gender, eg 'You're very analytical for a woman' or 'You're very sensitive for a man'. 1 2 3
C Responding to comments being made about your sexual orientation. 1 2 3
D Voicing your point of view on religion or politics. 1 2 3

6 Rights of mind

A Requesting service in a public place, when you have not received it, for example in a shop, restaurant, travel agent etc.   1 2 3
B Asking for feedback about your performance, on a work or personal project.   1 2 3
C Being alone in a medium-sized group when everyone else is with a partner.   1 2 3
D Feeling right about using your authority, without labelling yourself as 'impolite', 'aggressive', 'rude', 'parental' or 'bossy'.   1 2 3

Now add up your scores   **TOTAL ASSESSMENT 10 SCORE**

Ideally, you will now have completed all 10 assessments and tested your overall skills fitness. If so ➡ Fitness Profile p.35.

If, however, you have chosen to focus on understanding your individual response to stress ➡ About you Fitness Profile p.55.

Fitness Profile

Fitness Profile

Well done, you've completed Fitness Assessment – now you can find out the results!

Fitness Profile allows you to evaluate your current skills fitness – your strengths, weaknesses and priorities for action. It builds into a fitness profile unique to you.

Fitness profiles 1-3 relate directly to assessments 1-3. Similarly, profiles 4-8 and 9-10 relate to assessments 4-8 and 9-10.

Are you stressed?

Studies have shown that the first step in managing stress is to become aware of whether it is a problem for you (or not), and acknowledge this. The following three profiles will help you to assess the level of your stress symptoms.

PROFILE 1: PHYSICAL SIGNS

Look back to assessment 1 (p.5) and make a note of the number of boxes you ticked here ☐
For each box ticked ➡ **–1 POINT** SCORE

TOTAL ASSESSMENT 1 SCORE

TRAINER'S WARNING

It is advisable to seek medical help if you are experiencing ill health.

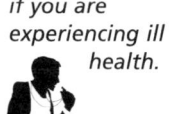

For assessment 1, the lower your score the greater your physical signs of stress. A higher score (ie one close to 0) would be healthier.
Your **lowest** score is **–22**.
Your **highest** score is **0**.

PROFILE 2: PSYCHOLOGICAL SIGNS

Look back to assessment 2 (p.6) and make a note of the number of boxes you ticked here ☐
For each boxed ticked ➡ **–1 POINT** SCORE

TOTAL ASSESSMENT 2 SCORE

For assessment 2, the lower your score the greater your psychological signs that may be stress related. Again, a score closer to 0 is healthier.
Your **lowest** score is **–22**.
Your **highest** score is **0**.

> **TRAINER'S WARNING**
>
> It is always advisable to seek the help of a trained counsellor or psychotherapist if you are experiencing ongoing mental ill health.

PROFILE 3: BEHAVIOURAL SIGNS

Look back to assessment 3 (p.7) and make a note of the number of boxes you ticked below.

Exercise 1 ☐
Exercise 2 ☐
Exercise 3 ☐

For each boxed ticked ➡ **–1 POINT**

Exercise 1 [SCORE]

Exercise 2 [SCORE]

Exercise 3 [SCORE]

EXERCISES 1 AND 2
Add your scores for exercises 1 and 2 together

For these two exercises the lower you score the greater your behavioural signs that may be stress related. Your **lowest** possible score for these two questions added together is **–16**. Your **highest** score is **0**.

EXERCISE 3
How you feel affects your body language. If you are feeling stressed, you may adopt inappropriate (ie non-assertive) body language.

Look back to exercise 3 (p.8); remind yourself of which body language you use.

Now see below to find out what this body language might be 'saying'.

A Little or no eye contact
The most likely interpretation is *avoiding* (submissive because you are unable to look assertively into somebody's eyes); it can also mean feeling emotions

B Shaking hands too hard, or too loose
Too hard may be seen as *aggressive*, which affects people's

reaction to you; too loose may be seen as submissive and *adapting*

C Pointing finger
The most likely interpretation here is that you will be perceived as being *aggressive* (accusative, critical)

D Twirling hair
The most likely interpretation is *appeasing* (anxious, childish, nervous)

E Hands on mouth
The most likely interpretation here is *adapting* (censoring, concerned at what is being said)

F Smiling too much
This is a sign of wanting to please and feeling that you need other people's approval (*appeasing*).

Remind yourself of your score. For this exercise, the lower you score the more likely it is that stress is affecting your body language. Your **lowest** score is **–6**, your **highest** score is **0**.

Now total up your scores for these three exercises

TOTAL ASSESSMENT 3 SCORE

> For assessment 3, the lower you score the more stressed you appear, and the more likely you are to affect others' stress levels.
> Your **lowest** score is **–22**.
> Your **highest** score is **0**.

So how healthy are your stress levels? Look back to p.39 for your score for
assessment 1 and write it down here ☐
Now your assessment 2 score ☐
Your assessment 3 score ☐

Add these individual scores together to make your **total are you stressed? score:**

SCORE

TOTAL ARE YOU STRESSED? SCORE

The lower your total score the more stressed you are, and the less your ability to manage your everyday causes of stress.
Your **lowest** possible score is **–66**.
Your **highest** score is **0**.

–20 to 0 Congratulations, you already have a healthy level of fitness and are relatively free of stress symptoms.

–43 to –21 You are moderately fit. You can be stress free at times but there are many warning signs to tell you to slow down. You could do with building your fitness.

–66 to –44 You are unfit! You need to do some work to address your stress levels.

Ideally, you should work through all 10 assessments, profiles and work-outs to improve your overall fitness. However, if you have chosen to focus on identifying potential signs of stress ➡ Are you stressed? work-out p.69. Before doing this, however, it is a good idea to do some quick mental preparation ➡ Warm-up p.63.

Sources of stress

The following five profiles will help you identify your sources of stress – at work and home.

PROFILE 4: WORK OR HOME STRESS?

Go back to p.9; remind yourself of the three exercises in assessment 4, and your responses. Make a note of your scores below.

Exercise 1 — SCORE

Exercise 2 — SCORE

Exercise 3 — SCORE

EXERCISE 1
Day-to-day stresses at work

For this question, the lower you score the more you find day-to-day experiences stressful. Your **lowest** score is **0**. Your **highest** score is **88**.

EXERCISE 2
Work 'events'

For this exercise, the lower you score the more potentially stressful work events you have experienced in the last 12 months. Your **lowest** score is **–296** your **highest** score is **0**.

EXERCISE 3
Life 'events'

For this exercise, the lower you score the more potentially stressful life events you have experienced in the last 12 months, and the greater your chance of experiencing negative health effects. Your **lowest** score is **–368** your **highest** score is **0**.

Now add together your scores for these three exercises

TOTAL ASSESSMENT 4 SCORE

> For assessment 4, the lower you score the more stressed you are.
> Your **lowest** possible score is **–664**.
> Your **highest** possible score is **88**.

PROFILE 5: TIME AND WORKLOAD MANAGEMENT

Look back at assessment 5 (p.16); remind yourself of the two exercises and your responses. Make a note of your scores below:

Exercise 1   SCORE

Exercise 2   A   SCORE

              B   SCORE

EXERCISE 1
Are you a 'workaholic'?
For this exercise, the lower you score the more likely you are to put too much emphasis on work. Get a life! Your **lowest** score is **0**. Your **highest** score is **42**.

EXERCISE 2
Do you have a time management problem?
For this exercise, the lower your 'A' score the greater your time management problems. Your **lowest** score is **0**, your **highest** score is **48**.

However, the lower your 'B' score the greater your time management skills.

Your **lowest** score is **0**, your **highest** score is **24**.

Now add together your score from exercise 1 and your 'A' score from exercise 2   TOTAL ASSESSMENT 5 SCORE

> For assessment 5, the lower your score the poorer your time and workload management skills. A higher score is healthier.
> Your **lowest** possible score is **0**, your **highest 90**.

PROFILE 6: COMMUNICATION

You tend to communicate better with people you like; you probably share a similar outlook on life and already 'speak the same language'. Look back to p.19 in Fitness Assessment. Remind yourself of exercises 1 and 2 and how you responded. Do any of the names you listed in question 1 also appear in your responses to question 2? If they do, make a note of their name below. Any surprises? Now check to see in which list (A or B) they appeared and tick the appropriate box below.

Name	**A**	**B**
....	☐	☐
....	☐	☐
....	☐	☐
....	☐	☐
....	☐	☐
....	☐	☐

Now answer the following questions.

		Yes	**No**
1	Did the people you like show up in Column A?	☐	☐
2	Did the people you dislike show up in column B?	☐	☐
3	Did the people you trust show up in Column A?	☐	☐
4	Did the people you distrust show up in column B?	☐	☐

5 Did the people you thought were promoted beyond their ability show up in column B? ☐ ☐
6 Did the people you have negative feelings towards show up in column B? ☐ ☐
7 Did the people you have positive feelings towards turn up in column A? ☐ ☐
8 Did the people you find sexually attractive show up in column A? ☐ ☐
9 Did the people you find intellectually stimulating show up in column A? ☐ ☐
10 Did you find that the people with a good sense of humour showed up in column A? ☐ ☐

Have you found that most of the people you feel positive about appear in column A and those you feel negative about in column B? Do you generally communicate better with people in column A than column B?

> There is no specific score for this assessment, however, you should be able to identify those people with whom you work and communicate well, and those with whom you work and communicate badly, and who cause you stress.

PROFILE 7: DEALING WITH PEOPLE

EXERCISE 1
Saying No to a particular person
Look back to p.21 in Fitness Assessment; remind yourself of the question and your responses. Write down the number of boxes you ticked here ☐
For each ticked box ➡ **−1 POINT** SCORE

For exercise 1 the lower you score the less able you are to say No to people. A higher score (closer to 0) is more healthy. Your **lowest** score is **−12**. Your **highest** score is **0**.

EXERCISE 2
Dealing with manipulation

Do you feel that the only way you can succeed in life is by manipulating and dominating people? Of course you don't! However, have you ever found yourself using some of the approaches described in the assessment?

Were you able to identify the different kinds of manipulation? Look back to p.23; remind yourself of the examples and your responses. Now write these responses (A-J) below.

Question 1 ☐
Question 2 ☐
Question 3 ☐
Question 4 ☐
Question 5 ☐
Question 6 ☐

So, how did you do?

1 'I realize that you're keen to get away for the weekend, but could you just do this photocopying for me before you leave?'
The preferred answer for question 1 is **B**. This comment is playing on your emotions

➡ **3 POINTS** SCORE

2 'You are the best public speaker we have, so I want you, rather than me, to give this presentation to the staff.'
The preferred answer for question 2 is **C**. This comment is appealing to your intellect

➡ **3 POINTS** SCORE

People try to manipulate you by working on certain perceived weaknesses. They may try to:
A Work on your vulnerabilities or 'crumple button'
B Appeal to your emotions
C Appeal to your intellect
D Hook your childhood messages
E Play on your friendship
F Use their status
G Appeal to your values
H Play on your loyalty
I Make you look foolish or put you down
J Get what they want, regardless of your needs.

3 'I recognize that you have to go to a funeral, however, you must be back by 4pm for this important meeting.'
The preferred answer for question 3 is **J**. This comment means the other person is getting what they want, regardless of your needs

➡ **3 POINTS** SCORE

4 'I know how loyal you are to me as your boss, so you have to attend the residential conference regardless of the difficulties you are having with your partner.'
The preferred answer for question 4 is **H**. This comment is playing on your loyalty

➡ **3 POINTS** SCORE

5 'I understand how disappointed you were when you didn't get the last promotion, but this will give you the opportunity to show how the wrong person was promoted.'
The preferred answer for question 5 is **A**. This comment is working on your vulnerabilities or 'crumple button'

➡ **3 POINTS** SCORE

6 'I expect you to refer all queries and ideas to me as your line manager before mentioning them to the directors.'
The preferred answer for question 6 is **F**. This comment is playing on status

➡ **3 POINTS** SCORE

Now add up your scores   SCORE

For exercise 2 the higher you score the better; the more able you are to listen to the 'music behind the words' and recognize when you are being manipulated.

Your **highest** score is **18**. Your **lowest** score is **0**.

Now total up your scores for exercises 1 and 2

TOTAL ASSESSMENT 7 SCORE

For assessment 7, the lower your score the less your ability to deal with people. A higher score is healthier. Your **highest** possible score is **18**.
your **lowest −12**.

PROFILE 8: DEALING WITH CONFLICT

EXERCISE 1
Your attitude to conflict

There are five main ways of dealing with conflict:
Avoiding (avoiding the issue or may be passing the buck)
Appeasing (saying 'everything will be all right')
Attacking (giving as good as you get)
Adapting ('agreeing' with the other person)
Addressing (making a judgement on the facts).

Which is your preferred style?
Look back to p.24 in Fitness Assessment; remind yourself of exercise 1, and how you responded (A-E). Make a note of your response here ☐

How did you do?
Your client complains to you about your overly bureaucratic system. What do you do?

A Agree with them about the stupid rules (*adapting*)
➡ **1 POINT**
B Tell them that they deserve to be delayed and that it's their fault (*attacking*) ➡ **0 POINTS**
C Ask them to tell you the facts of the case and then act on the evidence presented (*addressing*)
➡ **3 POINTS**

D Say 'It's nothing to do with me' (*avoiding*)

→ **0 POINTS**

E Say 'Don't worry, it will turn out all right' (*appeasing*)

→ **1 POINT**

SCORE

For this exercise, **C** is the preferred answer. You need to *address* conflict openly and calmly to minimize stress.

If you chose A (*adapting*) you may be able to calm the situation down in the short-term but you are storing up long-term stress if you don't soon address the issue.

If you chose B (*attacking*) you are aggressive and will create stress for both yourself and your colleagues.

If you chose D (*avoiding*) you may save yourself short-term stress but, again, are storing up trouble.

Finally, if you chose E (*appeasing*) you want to be liked. You are likely to be stressed if you are unable to address people and issues.

The higher your score for this exercise, the healthier your approach to conflict. Your **highest** score is **3**, your **lowest** score **0**.

EXERCISE 2
Identifying and managing conflict

So how did you do in exercise 2? Look back to p.25 and make a note of the options you ticked below (A-E).

Question 1 ☐
Question 2 ☐
Question 3 ☐
Question 4 ☐
Question 5 ☐

1 You are experiencing personal, family or relationship problems; you need to take some time off work (*inner conflict*). How do you react?

For question 1 the preferred answer is **E** – discuss with your line manager that you are having some personal difficulties and that it may be necessary to have some time away from work, which you will make up

➡ **3 POINTS** SCORE

2 You are receiving complaints from several members of your staff about the slackness of one of the team (*team conflict*). What do you do or say?
For this question the preferred answer is **E** – call the team together and ask them to voice their concerns about the 'team dynamics'

➡ **3 POINTS** SCORE

3 You have to make five redundancies (*organizational conflict*). How do you respond?
For question 3 the preferred answer is **D** – talk to all staff about the redundancies. Ask for volunteers first and then draw up a 'possibles' list, following consultation with staff and in the light of company regulations ➡ **3 POINTS** SCORE

4 Two of your staff have conflict between them. They each come separately to you and complain about the other (*conflict between two people for whom you have responsibility*). How do you deal with the problem?
A is the preferred response for this question: bringing the two members of staff together and asking them to tell each other what the issues are, and how they can be resolved ➡ **3 POINTS** SCORE

5 You are experiencing unjust treatment, bullying or harassment from someone at work (*conflict with one other person*). How do you respond?
The preferred answer for this question is **B** – talk to them about the behaviour that you have observed, tell

them how you feel and say what you need, in terms of their treatment of you

⟹ **3 POINTS** SCORE

Now add together your scores SCORE

For exercise 2 the higher you score the better able you are to manage conflict assertively, and minimize attendant stress. Your **highest** score is **15**. Your **lowest** score is **0**.

EXERCISE 3
Giving and receiving criticism

Look back to p.27 in Fitness Assessment and remind yourself of the situations and the options you circled. Give yourself 3 POINTS if you circled the options marked * below.

1 For the first time in months you are late for a one-to-one meeting. Your colleague exclaims 'You are always late for my meetings!' This is invalid (*unjustified*) criticism. How do you respond?

   A Walk away and get angry   1 2 3
   B Justify your behaviour   1 2 3
   C Ask for specific examples   1 2 3*

SCORE

2 You are being reprimanded in front of your colleagues (*public criticism*). How do you respond?

   A Say 'I don't think it is appropriate to discuss this with other people present.'   1 2 3*
   B Cry.   1 2 3
   C Blame other colleagues or circumstances.   1 2 3

SCORE

3 Your manager has recently cancelled two meetings with you at short notice. You are annoyed and complain to a director. Your manager is then upset to receive feedback from a director rather than from you first; she questions your behaviour. This is valid (*justified*) criticism. How do you react?

A Say 'Well, you are never here.' 1 2 3
B Say 'I'm sorry, you are right. It won't happen again.' 1 2 3*
C Say nothing, and then moan to your colleagues about what a rotten manager she is. 1 2 3

SCORE

4 Some of your colleagues are feeling de-motivated; you need to pass on some critical feedback to your manager. What do you say?

A 'Two members of the team are feeling very de-motivated, mainly because you hardly ever praise them for the extra work they do for you in their own time.' 1 2 3*
B 'Everyone in the team is de-motivated.' 1 2 3
C 'Everyone thinks that you're a useless manager.' 1 2 3

SCORE

Now add up your scores   SCORE

For exercise 3, the higher you score the better able you are to both give and receive criticism, and the less stressed you are. Your **highest** score is **12**. Your **lowest** score is **0**.

Now add together your scores for these three exercises

TOTAL ASSESSMENT 8 SCORE

> For assessment 8 the higher you score the better you are at dealing with conflict.
> Your **highest** possible score is **30**.
> Your **lowest** score is **0**.

So how fit are you at identifying your sources of stress?

Look back to p.43 for your score for assessment 4 and write it down here ☐

Now your assessment 5 score ☐

Now your assessment 7 score ☐

Finally, your assessment 8 score ☐

Add these individual scores together to make your **total sources of stress score**: TOTAL SOURCES OF STRESS SCORE

> The higher your total score the better able you are to identify, and manage, your sources of stress.
> Your **highest** possible score is **226**.
> your **lowest** score **–676**.

–74 to 226 Congratulations, you are able to manage your sources of stress and are relatively stress free. Are there any areas you could improve on?

–375 to –75 You are reasonably fit. You can identify some of your sources of stress and can be stress free at times, but there are many warning signs to tell you to slow down. You could do with building your fitness.

–676 to –376 You are not skills fit! You need to do some work on developing your ability to identify and understand your sources of stress.

Ideally, you should work through all 10 assessments, profiles and work-outs to improve your overall fitness. However, if you have chosen to focus on identifying your individual sources of stress ➡ Sources of stress work-out p.77. Before doing this, however, it is a good idea to do some quick mental preparation ➡ Warm-up p.63.

About you

The following two profiles will help you build up a picture of how – and why – you respond to stress in certain ways.

PROFILE 9: THINKING, FEELING AND BEHAVING

We have discussed the idea of 'creatures' sitting on your shoulder giving you messages about how you should think, feel or behave. They were put there when you were young. Whether your childhood experiences were essentially positive or negative, you were still given early behavioural messages – what and how to eat, what to wear etc. Some may have been positive and helpful like 'be happy', but others may have been unhelpful and had long-term negative effects such as you're 'no good at sports', 'a nasty, horrid person' or 'not as talented as your sister/brother.' As you have matured, some of these 'creatures' may have dropped off your shoulder; nonetheless, let's have a look to see if some are still hanging around.

Look back to assessment 9 (p.29-31) and make a note of your individual column scores below.

Column	A	B	C	D	E
	☐	☐	☐	☐	☐

> For this assessment, if you have a score of 3 or more in any one column you probably display a particular kind of behaviour (and have a particular 'creature' chattering to you on your shoulder). So, what do the columns tell you?

Column A – The 'Be Perfect' person
Column B – The 'Pleasing People' person
Column C – The 'Hurry Up' person
Column D – The 'Be Strong' person
Column E – The 'Try Harder' person

The Be Perfect person

Imagine the Be Perfect person lives in a room full of diamonds; diamond ceiling, floor and walls. Yet right in the corner is a load of manure. Instead of seeing the diamonds, the Be Perfect person focuses on the manure. Similarly, they tend to focus on what is wrong with someone rather than what is right. If you are a Be Perfect person you may play the psychological game of 'blemish', which is looking for the mistake rather than appreciating the whole. For example, someone hands you a finished project and your first reaction is 'There's a spelling mistake on page 90' instead of saying 'Thank you, there's a lot of good work gone into this. However, I am concerned about one or two spelling mistakes, let's get those right.'

As a child you were probably told to aim for perfection. Scripts like 'If a job's worth doing it's worth doing well'. So you tend to work at 100% all the time, rather than at 80%, which is achievable. Nobody is capable of working 100% all the time.

The Pleasing People person

If you have found this creature chatting to you, then you will probably nod a lot and smile, even when you don't agree with someone or feel upset! You are probably liked but may come across as ineffectual when it comes to sorting out conflict.

When you were small you were probably told 'Think about what the neighbours will say' or 'Be nice to people'. The message that you were picking up is that unless you are pleasant to people you are no good. Somehow you will be punished. So your style is to make others feel good so you can feel better. You find it really difficult to say No.

The Hurry Up person
Gosh, everything is such a rush for you. You are always busy doing so many things at once. Hurrying here hurrying there but still thinking about what else you ought to be doing instead. When you are in a meeting you think about whom you need to speak to at lunch. When you are at lunch you are thinking about being back in the meeting. You probably tap your fingers or twitch your leg more than most. Your speed is admirable but how are the people around you affected? They try to stop you in the corridor but you are in a hurry; 'I'll see you later' you reply, but 'later' you're still just as busy. You probably arrive late for meetings, letting everyone know how busy you've been. You can irritate others with your inability to listen and reflect.

As a child you were probably told to hurry up. 'We haven't got time to stand and wait, get on with it'; 'Hurry up, we need to be at your grandpa's in ten minutes.' This message may have stuck; though, more than likely, it's no longer appropriate.

The Be Strong person
You hardly ever have time off work and go in even when you are ill and others are off with the same condition. Not you; you're there rain or shine, in sickness and in health, never recognizing when you're tired or hungry, keeping going. You wait until the weekend or holidays to be ill.

When you were small you were probably told to be strong and keep your feelings to yourself. Sayings like 'Big boys don't cry'; 'Put on a brave face'; 'Don't let them know that you are hurting.'

The Try Harder person
If you have found that your internal dialogue is about trying harder then you are probably always searching for something

else. Just take stock of what is good about *this* job, *this* relationship. Ask yourself: 'For whom am I trying harder?' You may always be looking to the future but you need to be happy in the here and now and ask for what you need now.

As a child you were well versed in 'could do better' and were often compared with brothers, sisters, cousins or others. Maybe you came home from school and said 'I came second in the science test' only to be asked 'Who came first?' You were always expected to try harder. 'Do your best' is the mantra, but when you have done your best and still not received the approval of 'well done' then that really is hard.

> There is no final score for this assessment, however you should now have a valuable insight into how your early childhood messages affect your behaviour.

PROFILE 10: ASSERTIVENESS

Look back to assessment 10 (p.31); remind yourself of the situations and your responses. Make a note of your score here   SCORE

> For assessment 10 the higher you score the more confident you feel about people and situations, and the more naturally assertive you behave.
> Your **highest** score is **72**.
> Your **lowest** score is **24**.

Like most people, there are probably situations where you behave less assertively than others. Having identified these areas, concentrate on how you can improve your skills to handle these occasions more appropriately.

If you want to be able to manage your stress you need to

be assertive. Remember, assertive behaviour is about being open, honest, focused and direct. Non-assertive behaviour is either appeasing or aggressive.

Check out the '3 A's' spectrum below and see how you fare.

	Appeasing	**Assertive**	**Aggressive**
Speech	Quiet Unsure, indirect: 'May', 'If possible', 'Would you mind?' or 'Can I just say?'	Clearly audible Direct and concise: 'I need', 'want', 'have'	Loud Accusative (battle language!): 'Should', 'Will', 'Ought'
Eyes	Lowered	Straight gaze	Glaring
Body language	Hunched, withdrawn, rigid, shoulders stooped	Upright, shoulders down, 'open' gestures	Pointed finger, hands on hips, fingers forward, curled fists, chin forward
Feelings	Fear, guilt, inadequacy, insecure, unsure	Confident, self-love, calm, democratic	Anger, frustration, revenge, autocratic
Attitudes	'Could do better', like to please, easily persuaded, my fault!	'I know what I need', prepared to listen and to find out the needs of others	'Don't argue with me', think they are right, stubborn!
Early childhood messages	Turn the other cheek. Don't push yourself forward. Be nice	As good as anyone else You are special You are loved	Stand up for yourself. Don't let anyone win. Give as good as you get
See themselves	As inferior	As an equal	As superior

So how healthy is your response to stress, and your understanding of why you behave in this way? Make a note of your assessment 10 score here ☐

This makes your **total about you score**:

TOTAL ABOUT YOU SCORE

The higher your total score the more you understand how and why you respond to stress in certain ways, and the more positive this response.
Your **highest** possible score is **72**.
Your **lowest** score **24**.

58 to 72 Congratulations, you already have a healthy level of fitness and respond to stress positively.

41 to 57 You are moderately fit. You can manage your stress at times but need to build your overall fitness.

24 to 40 You are not skills fit. You need to do some work on improving your individual response to stress.

Ideally, you should now have worked through all 10 assessments and profiles. If so, turn to the following page to discover your **overall stress management fitness level**.

If, however, you have chosen to focus on understanding, and working on, your individual response to stress ➡ About you work-out p.91. Before doing this, though, you should do some quick mental preparation ➡ Warm-up p.63.

How good are you at stress management?

You should now have completed all 10 assessments and profiles, and have a good idea of how fit you are in stress management.

Personal fitness profile

Look back at how you scored in the three sections:
Are you stressed?
Sources of stress, and
About you.

Make a note of your individual total scores for these sections below:

Are you stressed?	☐
Sources of stress	☐
About you	☐
What is your total stress management score?	☐

TOTAL STRESS MANAGEMENT SCORE

−40 to 298 Congratulations, you are reasonably fit. Are there any areas you could improve still further?

−379 to −41 You are moderately fit. You could do with building your ability to manage stress.

−718 to −380 You are not fit! You need to do some work to build your understanding, awareness and skills.

Now take another look at your individual total scores for the three sections. Circle these scores overleaf.

	UNFIT	**REASONABLY FIT**	**FIT**
Are you stressed?	−66 to −44	−43 to −21	−20 to 0
Sources of stress	−676 to −376	−375 to −75	−74 to 226
About you	24 to 40	41 to 57	58 to 72

Are you strong or weak in any particular section/skills area? Are you, for example, strong when it comes to identifying your causes of stress, but weak when actually dealing with them? Or perhaps you have strengths and weaknesses across all sections? Look back at your individual scores in profiles 1–10. Can you identify any particular strengths or weaknesses?

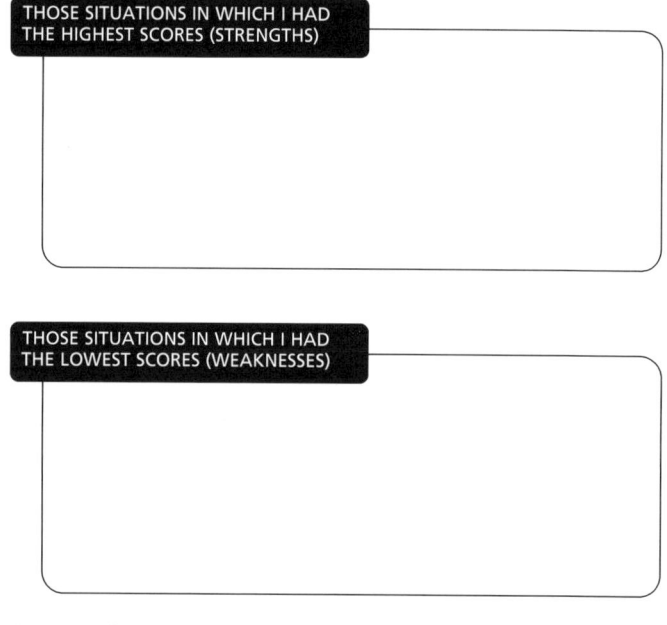

THOSE SITUATIONS IN WHICH I HAD THE HIGHEST SCORES (STRENGTHS)

THOSE SITUATIONS IN WHICH I HAD THE LOWEST SCORES (WEAKNESSES)

Congratulations on your strengths, but you do need to take action to develop your weaker areas.

Before moving on to Work-out, you need to do some quick mental preparation ➡ Warm-up p.63.

Warm-up

It is a good idea to do a quick mental warm-up before tackling the exercises in Work-out. Take a few moments now to reflect on your reasons for wanting to manage your stress better, identifying any benefits it will bring you and others. Now think about what it might be like to manage your stress effectively, to feel more relaxed, more in harmony with yourself and your thinking. Imagine a particular situation where you are managing stress well...

What do you look like?
My eye contact is ....
My body posture is ....

What do you sound like/what are you saying?
The tone of my voice is ....
I am saying ....

How are others reacting [positively] to you?
Others are saying ....
Others are being ....

How are you feeling?
I am feeling ....

You are now ready to make this a reality. If you have completed all 10 assessments and profiles ➡ Work-out p.65. If, however, you have chosen to focus on a particular skills area/section

➡ Are you stressed? work-out p.69
➡ Sources of stress work-out p.77
➡ About you work-out p.91

Work-out

Work-out

So, you've had your Fitness Assessment and identified your strengths and areas on which you need to work. Now it's time to take action!

Packed with practical exercises and activities, Work-out contains all the equipment you need to become super-fit at stress management.

Look back at your personal fitness profile on p.61. Where do your strengths and weaknesses lie? Do they lie in specific areas of the skill – are you, for example, generally strong when it comes to identifying your sources of stress but weak when it comes to actually dealing with them? Or do they relate to all three skills areas? Depending on your personal fitness profile, you can either focus on improving a particular area of skill or work on individual weaknesses within each area.

Of course, if you want to raise your level of performance in all areas complete all the activities, then you really will be super-fit!

Work-outs 1-3 relate directly to fitness profiles 1-3. Similarly, work-outs 4-8 and 9-10.

Are you stressed?

In order to manage stress, you first need to understand how it is currently affecting you – physically, psychologically and behaviourally. You then need to take action to minimize these effects. The following three work-outs will help you to achieve this.

WORK-OUT 1: PHYSICAL SIGNS

The following tips will help you deal with or minimize the physical symptoms of stress. They will also help stop you developing these symptoms in the first place.

- ✓ Take regular exercise – at least 20 minutes a couple of times a week. Walking is relatively easy to fit into a schedule. Also, many sports offer ways in which to rid the body of tension and can release turned-in aggression.
- ✓ Eat a balanced diet. Eat slowly and sit down, allowing at least half an hour for each meal. Avoid excessive caffeine, alcohol and fat.
- ✓ The very nature of stress may mean that you find it hard to relax. You may think that relaxing is a waste of your already short time. However, finding time and space each day to relax is important. Identify how you currently relax, maybe it's just putting your feet up in front of the TV or having a bath. Think about trying new ways to relax such as yoga, aromatherapy or reflexology.
- ✓ In order to get a good night's sleep try

There are two major parts of the central nervous system that affect your physical response to stress:
The sympathetic nervous system *– this governs the pituitary gland that can activate the adrenal glands, stimulating a 'fight', 'flight' or 'fright' response. Can cause palpitations, hyperventilation, stomach upsets, sweaty palms, cold feet and muscular spasms.*
The parasympathetic nervous symptom *– this governs the digestive process and tissue repair.*

having a warm drink (no caffeine) and/or a warm bath. If you wake early then get up rather than spend time worrying about not sleeping. Look forward to going to bed; it could be the only time you have to enjoy being alone with your thoughts.
✓ Try and breathe slowly and calmly; say 'relax' to yourself as you breathe out.

WORK-OUT 2: PSYCHOLOGICAL SIGNS

People respond differently to pressure; they are conditioned by how they think and feel about situations and people. If you change your attitude you may find you can change your responses.

Reframing your attitude

A useful technique here is 'reframing'. When you are feeling stressed, think or say to yourself 'What a wonderful opportunity to...' This puts the situation in a positive light, and you in a position of being able to influence events.

A step on from this is actually to begin a sentence with 'What a wonderful opportunity to...', so if something happens that is unexpected, inconvenient, hurtful or difficult, try 'reframing' in this way.

Start with today. You may be thinking and feeling that working on this book is a waste of your time. You may think that you have better and more important things to be doing or you may have felt compelled to do this either by 'management', your colleagues or partner. Whatever frame of mind you are in at present, try and 'reframe' your attitude; think objectively about your priorities, then say to yourself 'What a wonderful opportunity to...........................'

What's the worst thing that could happen?
Another useful technique is to ask yourself: What's the worst thing that could happen? Often, the worst thing simply

doesn't happen and, even if it does, it's usually not as bad as you think or you find you have the skills and abilities to deal with it.

Challenging irrational thinking

The way we think, our belief and value systems may also add to our stress levels – if they are unrealistic, perhaps even irrational. Below is a list of statements that are essentially irrational, and which encourage emotional disturbance and stress. Read through these statements carefully, ticking any that reflect your attitude.

1 'I need approval! I must – yes, must – have love or approval from all the people I find significant, otherwise I cannot approve of myself.' ☐
2 'I must be competent! I must prove thoroughly competent, adequate and achieving' or (a saner but still foolish variation) 'I at least must have competence or talent in some important area, otherwise I am worthless.' ☐
3 'People are bad! When people act obnoxiously and unfairly I should blame them and damn them, and see them as bad or rotten individuals.' ☐
4 'My life is full of disasters! I view things as awful, terrible, horrible and catastrophic when I get seriously frustrated, treated unfairly or rejected, or when people and things don't turn out the way they should.' ☐
5 'I cannot change how I feel! Emotional misery comes from external pressures and I have little ability to control or change my feelings.' ☐
6 'I must worry about what might happen! If something seems dangerous or fearsome I must preoccupy myself with it, make myself anxious about it or keep dwelling on the possibility of it recurring.' ☐
7 'It is better to avoid rather than address my issues and concerns! I can more easily avoid facing many of life's difficulties and responsibilities than take a potentially

more rewarding path with its attendant risks.' ☐
8. 'I need someone to look after me! I have to be dependent on others and need someone stronger than myself to lean on.' ☐
9. 'What has happened to me will always affect me! My past remains all-important, and because something once strongly influenced my life it has to keep determining my feelings and behaviour today.' ☐
10. 'I should always worry about others! I should be quite upset by other people's problems, concerns or worries and should carry these problems with me.' ☐

(Adapted by Jeanie Civil from Rational Emotive Behaviour Therapy by Albert Ellis.)

Now, try to change the following statements into more positive, helpful concepts. (The first one has been completed as an example.)

1. 'I need approval! I must – yes must – have love or approval from all the people I find significant, otherwise I cannot approve of myself' *can be changed to* 'I love me and approve of myself; if I gain other people's approval, then that's a bonus.'
2. 'I must be competent! I must prove thoroughly competent, adequate and achieving' or (a saner but still foolish variation) 'I at least must have competence or talent in some important area, otherwise I am worthless' *can be changed to* ....
....
3. 'People are bad! When people act obnoxiously and unfairly I should blame them and damn them, and see them as bad or rotten individuals' *can be changed to*
....
4. 'My life is full of disasters! I view things as awful, terrible, horrible and catastrophic when I get seriously frustrated, treated unfairly or rejected, or when people

and things don't turn out the way they should' *can be changed to* ....
5. 'I cannot change how I feel! Emotional misery comes from external pressures and I have little ability to control or change my feelings' *can be changed to* ....
....
6. 'I must worry about what might happen! If something seems dangerous or fearsome I must preoccupy myself with it, make myself anxious about it or keep dwelling on the possibility of it recurring' *can be changed to* .....
....
7. 'It is better to avoid rather than address my issues and concerns! I can more easily avoid facing many of life's difficulties and responsibilities than take a potentially more rewarding path with its attendant risks' *can be changed to* ....
8. 'I need someone to look after me! I have to be dependent on others and need someone stronger than myself to lean on' *can be changed to* ....
....
9. 'What has happened to me will always affect me! My past remains all-important, and because something once strongly influenced my life it has to keep determining my feelings and behaviour today' *can be changed to* ....
10. 'I should always worry about others! I should be quite upset by other people's problems, concerns or worries and should carry these problems with me' *can be changed to* ....

Have some fun!

Be spontaneous, natural and free. Try and enjoy the simple pleasures of life. Have a laugh; laughter is a great stress reliever, it increases the body's level of endorphins which can help 'ease the pain'.

WORK-OUT 3: BEHAVIOURAL SIGNS

Stress can adversely affect your behaviour – not only what you do, but also how you speak, sound and look. You need to adopt assertive behaviour. Here are some tips.

Speech
✓ Speak audibly and calmly, not too fast or too slow. Speaking quietly and slowly could be perceived as patronizing, speaking loudly as aggressive.
✓ Avoid finishing off other people's sentences; not only is this rude, it can also be intimidating.
✓ Watch your tone of voice as well as your words. You may be using the right words but be coming across as aggressive by speaking in an abrupt, clipped way.

Body language
In face-to-face communication, what you say accounts for 7% of someone's impression of you, your voice 38% and body language 55%. This is why paying attention to what you *do* rather than what you say is so important.

> **TRAINER'S WARNING**
> *Beware of giving out unconscious, conflicting messages. For example, saying something complimentary to someone but pointing your finger at the same time may be perceived as aggressive or critical.*

Whatever the situation, you need to appear confident and assertive, even though inwardly you may be feeling anxious, nervous or stressed. You need to send out positive body language signals; if necessary, 'Fake it till you make it!'

In order to be assertive you need to be aware of how the different parts of your body can 'talk' to other people, and how you can present a congruent, assertive image. Profile 3 on p.40 gave some pointers as to what different body language might be 'saying'. Here we explore body language, and its implications, further.

Remember, there are cultural differences in different parts of the world. Some of the gestures I refer to are multi-cultural, others may just belong to the Western world. For example, people of different nationalities may have different personal spaces. Some people will naturally move very close to the person to whom they are speaking (eg in the UK), whereas others might regard this as unacceptable behaviour. As might showing the under sole of your shoe or looking into the eyes of someone older or wiser than yourself. Within the same culture there will be some people who have different preferences for body gestures; some individuals will like to be touched, others will shy away from physical contact of any kind.

Body talk
Ask a friend or colleague to sit down with you in a quiet room and have a 10-minute, two-way conversation about a specific issue. Imagine the meeting is quite formal; shake hands when you enter the room. Now think about how your body 'talked' during this conversation.

Head and face talk
How did you hold your head? How did you use your eyes and mouth? Ask your friend what they think.

To be assertive you need to:
- ✓ Hold your head at the same angle as the person to whom you are speaking.
- ✓ Look straight at the person speaking when you are listening.
- ✓ Smile only when you are genuinely pleased. Assertive people smile when pleased, not to please.

What can you do with your head and face to look assertive?

Arm and shoulder talk
Now think about how you used your arms and shoulders. Lifted shoulders can mean 'I don't know what you're talking about.' Arms folded can mean 'I'm uncomfortable' or 'I don't want to be here.' How did you use your arms and shoulders?

To look assertive, try and keep your shoulders relaxed and your arms below your shoulders.

Hand talk

How did you use your hands? First let's consider your handshake. An aggressive, dominant handshake is one where the palm is lowered over and on top of the other person's. To shake hands assertively take your hand as far up to the other person's thumb as you can. Shake firmly; there is nothing worse than a wet fish! Equally, don't shake hands with a vice-like grip. What sort of handshake did you have? Can you develop a more assertive handshake?

How else did you use your hands? Open, relaxed hands show acceptance. 'Steepling' of hands, however, could indicate a 'know it all' or patronizing attitude.

Leg and feet talk

If you cross your arms and legs you look hard to convince. It could also indicate displeasure.

Now think about your feet. Feet can be a big give away. Turned-up feet could indicate that you are uncomfortable. This gesture is called 'crying with the feet'. So, keep your feet firmly on the ground, and try not to wriggle them.

Posture talk

How you sit on the chair can indicate various things... If you lean forward then this is an invasion of the other person's space. You look as if you are ready to finish talking to them. If you sit with one arm hooked over the back of a chair this may be giving the impression 'I really don't want to be here.' How did you sit? What was your posture? To be assertive you need to adopt an open, accepting posture. Don't invade someone else's space or give off unhelpful signals. Try and keep as still as possible; stillness is empowering.

There may be many reasons for people moving their bodies in certain ways. If you want to be assertive then a good rule of thumb is to sit in an 'open' body position while keeping as still as you possibly can; this will make the other person feel more relaxed and comfortable in your presence. Recognize that your body language may be sending out negative messages, which could be entirely opposite to those you intend. If you think this applies to you, then remember the old tip, 'Fake it till you make it!'

Are you stressed? checklist

✓ Learn how to relax your mind and body.
✓ Take regular exercise, at least 20 minutes a couple of times a week.
✓ Think positively; challenge irrational thinking.
✓ Adopt assertive speech and body language.

Sources of stress

WORK-OUT 4: WORK OR HOME STRESS?

You can get stressed out by people and events at both work and home. Some can be day-to-day happenings, others specific events. Below are some useful tips and techniques to help you deal with the stresses and strains of life.

Facing up to stress

There are five main generic causes of stress:

1 The perception of the demand placed upon us.
2 An imbalance between the amount of challenge and the amount of support.
3 One bit of our lives is taking up more time and energy than it should, to the detriment of another part.
4 When we are asked to do something that challenges our values.
5 When we are experiencing major change.

Below, write down five things that are currently causing you stress.

> **TRAINER'S WARNING**
>
> *Be realistic, if you cannot change anything for now, you need to accept it and move on.*

1 ....
2 ....
3 ....
4 ....
5 ....

Look at these 'stressors'; can you do anything about them? Can you remove the cause of the stress by addressing the issue openly (check out work-out 10)? Can you minimize its effects?

> **TRAINER'S WARNING**
>
> *It is unwise to rely on just one person to provide support; it can put a strain on them and your relationship.*

Building up your support network

During times of stress, it is important that you are not over-independent or self-reliant. Talking to someone you trust can help put things into perspective and provide valuable insights. Bottling up emotion rarely helps, and usually ends up exacerbating stress.

Identify your support network by completing the following.

Question	Who?
Who can I rely on in a crisis?	
Who makes me feel good about myself?	
Who can I be totally myself with?	
Who can give me honest feedback in a way that I can hear?	
Who can I talk to when I am worried about work?	
Who can I talk to when I am worried about home?	
Who is able to make me stop and think about what I am doing?	
Who helps me to put things into perspective?	
Who introduces me to new ideas, people and opportunities?	

Regaining control

If you are confronted with a moment of stress, and need to gather yourself together, try and think of a place where you feel calm and safe – maybe lying on a beach listening to the waves, maybe walking through the woods seeing the flowers, trees and wildlife. Imagine yourself there, let the feelings of warmth and peace flow over you. Once you have regained your equilibrium, try and hang on to that sense of peace and calm as you face the stressful situation.

WORK-OUT 5: TIME AND WORKLOAD MANAGEMENT

In today's business culture you are often expected to do more with less. This can be very stressful. You need to take control of your time and workload before it overwhelms you. Remember, we all get 168 hours per week – it's how you use them that counts. Below are some handy tips.

Prioritizing your work

Tasks can be broken down into one of four categories:
1. Important and urgent
2. Urgent but not important
3. Important and not urgent
4. Neither urgent nor important.

Do those tasks that are important and urgent first, urgent but not important second, important and not urgent third, and don't do the not urgent and not important ones at all if you can help it! If faced with two tasks of equal importance, do the harder one first.

Planning
- ✓ Plan your time; don't let it control you.
- ✓ Create a rolling 'to do' list. A 'to do' list involves planning as you go along. Essentially, either in your diary or on your computer (if it has a 'to do' facility), every time you think of something that needs to be

done write it down on the day on which you intend to do it. For example, if you remember you need to confirm a meeting, but not until the 11th (and today is the 2nd) then simply turn to the 11th of the month and make a note. You can forget about it until the 11th, when you look at that particular page in the diary.
- ✓ Use a memo book for your notes. You're worth having a book as a reference, not just bits and scraps of paper.
- ✓ Tick each task as you complete it to give yourself a sense of achievement.

Delegation
- ✓ Delegate wherever possible. Remember to tell the person to whom you delegate that they are competent and confident.
- ✓ Delegate upwards, downwards and sideways.
- ✓ When delegating, delegate the power with the job. Avoid poking your nose in at times when you haven't agreed to do so.
- ✓ Always give or agree a final completion date.

Saying No
If you can't delegate or can't say No, you may end up overstretched, and overstressed. Remember, when saying No:
- ✓ Avoid being deliberately unhelpful – offer alternatives if you can.
- ✓ Briefly and clearly state what you are *not* willing to do followed up with a statement about what you *are* willing to do, if appropriate.
- ✓ Avoid making profuse apologies.
- ✓ Offer an explanation if necessary, but avoid over-justification.
- ✓ Keep it short and simple.
- ✓ Avoid personalizing your refusal.
- ✓ If pressed, repeat your refusal, slowing down and stressing important words.

Filing

- ✓ Get rid of your desk trays! You should have only two trays on your desk – the first labeled 'In' the other 'Filing'. Empty the 'In' tray at least twice a day, the filing tray every day. Put things away; have a clear desk.
- ✓ You really don't need to keep paper file copies of most documents. The originator should keep a copy if it's important. Every time you are considering filing something, ask yourself: What's the worst thing that could happen if this file didn't exist? Am I the only person who has this information (who else has a copy?) Is there a legal requirement to keep a paper copy? As a general rule, you should not need to file more than about 10% of paperwork you receive. If you have scanning facilities then scan in any documents that you don't need paper copies of for legal reasons. Otherwise, the rule with filing is Read, Reply, Reject (ie bin!).
- ✓ Colour code different types of file, eg red for budgets.
- ✓ If something has not been used for a year then throw it away – if in doubt, throw it out.

Using the telephone

- ✓ Negotiate with a colleague that they answer the phone when you need uninterrupted time.
- ✓ Arrange a specific call back time. Don't just say 'I'll ring back' or, even worse, 'Get them to ring me later.'
- ✓ If leaving a message, give your name, telephone number, when you'll be available and a brief description of the reason for ringing.
- ✓ Leave messages on answer phones in the same way.
- ✓ If interrupted by a telephone call, make a brief note of what you are thinking or writing at the time so that you can go straight back to completing the task.
- ✓ Cross-index your telephone directory.
- ✓ Get to the point. It's pleasant to socialize, but avoid wasting a lot of time.

Meetings
- ✓ Have meetings when they are necessary, not just because it is 'Wednesday'.
- ✓ Prepare for meetings – get hold of the agenda; clarify the purpose of the meeting (and whether you need to be there for all of it); do whatever preparation you need to do (eg reading up on any paperwork, highlighting relevant points).
- ✓ Attend the meeting for the item for which you need to be present, rather than sit through the entire meeting (check timings on the agenda).
- ✓ Ask yourself: Are the right people at the meeting?
- ✓ Always check at the end of the meeting what everyone thinks they are going away to do.
- ✓ Write brief records stating who is to complete what 'action'.

Making time for you
It is important to make time for yourself so you can recharge your batteries and minimize the effects of stress. This can be some time each day or some time each week.

Divide up this pie with the time you currently spend in one week on work, family, friends, hobbies/sports, household chores and simply yourself.

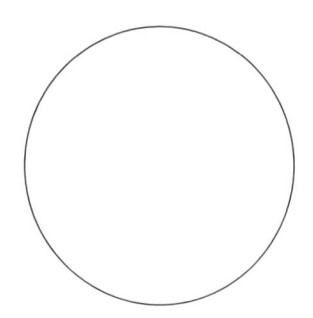

> **TRAINER'S WARNING**
>
> *Be sure to take your holiday entitlement. Try to plan at least one holiday each year with a change of activities or surroundings.*

Are you surprised by the results? Would you like to make any changes? Now divide up the pie how you would like it to be.

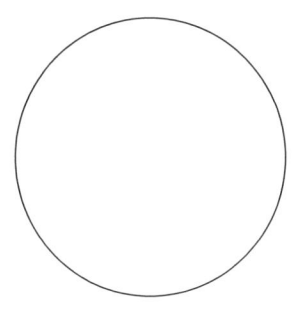

What are you going to do in order to achieve these changes?
1 ....
2 ....
3 ....
4 ....

WORK-OUT 6: COMMUNICATION

How you communicate with people can affect both how others respond to you and how you as an individual feel – stressed or relaxed.

Using different words and language can make a tremendous difference to how you are perceived, and how you feel about yourself. Develop a strategy to improve your self-worth by changing sentences beginning with:

Should into *could*
Must into *might*
Have to into *choose to*
Ought to into *prefer to*.

This language gives you more choices, improves your sense of control and lessens any sense of guilt! We can use words like 'should', 'must', 'have to' and 'ought to' as a stick to beat ourselves with, denying ourselves choices of action. Get rid of this stress!

Use assertive language – 'I wish to say'; 'I believe'; 'I think' and 'feel'; 'I need to listen' *not* 'Can I just say?' or 'Can I add to what you've just said?' This rings of permission, sounding like 'Can I just have a little breath of your air?'

The language people use can directly affect how you react to that person. You may well object to swearing or defamatory comments about work or home, but often it is subtler than that. Speech might include using certain words that create a feeling of unease or stress. For example, using words like:

Working '*for*' people instead of working '*with*' them
'*Confronting*' or '*tackling*' people instead of '*addressing*'
'*Problems*' instead of '*issues*' or '*concerns*'
'*Why*' instead of '*what*' or '*how*'.

What words create negative feelings in you? Think about how you could make your responses more assertive through language.

Reframing your language

Our language can create stress in others or inform people how stressed we are. We may use battle language – 'I fought for the section', 'The knives are out'; or catastrophic language – 'It was a nightmare', 'The effects will be horrendous', 'No one's job will be safe'.

One way of handling stress is to learn to 'reframe' your language. This means turning negative thoughts or statements into positive statements.

For example:
Your line manager says to you: 'I would like you to take over the administration of this particular project because you are a good organizer.'
You reply: 'Yes, OK' (but really you want to say NO).

Thought: There he/she goes again, always asking me to do the paperwork, why do I always get lumbered instead of other staff?

Reframing: It feels really good that I am considered to be so capable; however, I must ensure that if I take on this extra administration I will drop some other area of work or secure some support, otherwise I will overload myself. Also, I could ask my line manager to indicate what he/she thinks is my priority.

Now think of a particular situation that has happened to you at work: ....
....
....

Now try to 'reframe' your natural responses: ....
....
....

WORK-OUT 7: DEALING WITH PEOPLE

How other people behave (and how you respond) will affect you, and your stress levels. In order to minimize stress, you need to *address* people and issues openly and directly, you need to behave assertively.

Saying No to a particular person

Some people can really stress you out. Maybe you feel intimidated by them, maybe you want to impress them or gain their approval. Whatever the reason, remember that you are entitled to say No, but you may need to work on your assertiveness skills to achieve this.

- ✓ Use simple direct language, repeat the point if necessary. You can say 'sorry' if you like, but don't over-apologize.
- ✓ Demonstrate that you are hearing what the other person is saying, and empathize with their position.

However, if you really cannot help (and cannot offer a suitable compromise), say No again.

Dealing with manipulation

Remember, when people use manipulation they are looking for a pay-off. People try to manipulate you by working on certain psychological 'triggers' or perceived weaknesses. They may, for example, try to appeal to your emotions or to your intellect. They may play on your loyalties or their status. Whatever they do, the 'broken record' technique can help you handle the situation.

The 'broken record' technique

The phrase 'broken record' means continually repeating a clear statement of your needs and wishes. You should acknowledge the other person's point of view, but then repeat your point assertively. In effect, you will sound like an old gramophone record when the needle gets stuck in the groove and keeps repeating the same phrase over and over again.

The 'broken record' technique is probably the most basic skill you need to handle manipulative behaviour. By using this technique, combined with positive body language and concise spoken language, you can stop the manipulator achieving their goal.

Use the following model to help you respond to manipulation assertively.

When you ....
(comment on the other person's behaviour)
The *effect* on me is ....
(state concisely how their behaviour affects your life or your feelings)
I *feel* ....(share your feelings)
I *need* ....(ask for what you need).

It can be helpful to begin with 'I'm finding this hard to say, however…' Fear can prevent you from responding assertively. Recognize that you have emotional rights and that, whatever your status or salary, you are equal in terms of emotions. Try to reduce competitive feelings. Decide on your goals and be true to your values. You can always try to ask the other person for their thoughts and feelings on a situation. Ask them to empathize with how you are likely to be feeling in that situation.

If the manipulator looks upset or tearful, you can say 'I'm sorry you feel upset, however, I needed to be honest with you.' If they become angry, then you could say 'I think we need to discuss this at a later stage.'

Think of something that has been said to you that you now recognize was manipulative. Replay the situation in your mind; try to respond assertively using these phrases:

When you ....
The effect on me is ....
I feel ....
I need ....

WORK-OUT 8: DEALING WITH CONFLICT

You may dislike conflict, but resolving it assertively can bring positive outcomes. The following work-out offers you practical tips and advice for dealing, in a less stressful way, with conflict.

Different ways of handling conflict

Look back to exercises 1 and 2 in assessment 8; remind yourself of the different forms conflict can take, and how you responded to the different scenarios. Now look back to profile 8 on p.49. How did you deal with conflict; did you face the conflict openly and calmly or did you try and hide from it? What was your preferred style?

People's styles depend on how important goals and

> **TRAINER'S WARNING**
> Deal with conflict as it arises, don't delay.

relationships are to them. Ideally, you need to aim to *address* conflict.

You need to:
- ✓ Separate the issue from the person.
- ✓ Clarify the issues; share your perceptions of the conflict and the desired outcome.
- ✓ Take one issue at a time and avoid using examples from the past (this can lead to distortion and manipulation since the other person is likely to have forgotten the incident or remember it differently).
- ✓ Be honest about your needs and feelings. Use clear 'I' statements; this takes responsibility for yourself and avoids blaming other people for how you feel.
- ✓ Remember, this is not about winning or losing. You need to work towards a win-win outcome together. Brainstorming ideas can sometimes help.

> **TRAINER'S WARNING**
> Bullies and harassers tend not to target people who are assertive. If these behaviours persist, however, you will need to tell your line manager, or their superior.

Think of a situation where you were involved in conflict (it might be simplest if you recall a situation where you were in conflict with just one other person). How did you react? Did you behave assertively? If yes, then well done! If no, then replay the situation in your mind, but this time try to address the situation; behave assertively.

Giving and receiving criticism

Receiving criticism

How do you react to criticism? Some people start to justify their behaviour, others say nothing but feel angry or upset. Others respond by blaming someone else. There will be times when you are criticized, so

> **TRAINER'S TIP**
> You are allowed to make mistakes so, if valid, admit them! Using humour, eg 'That's the first mistake I ever made!', can help diffuse tension.

it is important that you are able to handle criticism in a way that is productive to both you and the critic.

Think of an example when someone has criticized you:
1 What exactly did they say? ....
2 How did you respond? ....
3 What was the outcome? ....

Now ask yourself:
1 Was the criticism valid (justified) or invalid (unjustified)?
   ....
2 If it was valid criticism, did you agree with them? ....
   ....
3 If it was invalid criticism, did you disagree with what the person said and say why it was invalid? ....
   ....
4 Was the criticism vague? ....
5 Did you ask them to give you specific examples of their criticism of your behaviour? ....
6 Who had the problem? ....
7 What could you do differently next time? ....
   ....

So, how *should* you respond to criticism? First of all you will need to decide if the criticism is valid or invalid. If it is valid, then you should admit this and agree. If not, then you should say so and explain why it is invalid.

However, what often happens is:
Critic: 'You never meet deadlines!'
You: 'Oh yes I do, it's just that you expect more and more of me and if I had more resources then I could get the job done quicker. It's impossible trying to work to deadlines here because so many staff are either off sick or are sent to work off-site and nobody knows where they are or when they are returning. I can never get in touch with them to get the information I require to finish my report...' and so on.

You have resorted to defending and justifying your behaviour. Remember that you have the following options.

VALID	INVALID		
Agree	Say it's invalid and why	Ask for specific examples	Who's got the problem?
Apologize and explain. This takes the heat out of the situation.	Perhaps there is a misunderstanding.	Criticism needs to be focused.	Say 'I can see that this is a problem for you.' This should be the last resort, try the other suggestions first.

Giving criticism

As well as receiving criticism, you may sometimes have to give critical feedback to others. When doing this:
- ✓ Be specific; give examples rather than being vague.
- ✓ Comment on a person's *behaviour* (which can be changed) rather than their personality (which can't).
- ✓ Recognize that *you* may be wrong and that the other person could have a good and valid reason for what has happened; you will not know unless you ask them.
- ✓ Recognize your prejudices and stereotyping.
- ✓ Most people deal with conflict in one of five main ways, from avoiding to attacking. Learn to *address* conflict.

Sources of stress checklist

✓ Identify your sources of stress, and what you can or cannot do about them.
✓ Prioritize your work and plan your time.
✓ Delegate and learn to say No.
✓ Practise reframing your language to empower yourself and minimize stress in other people.
✓ Address conflict openly, and early!

About you

Even though you may feel tired and stressed, you do have the resources to turn things around. The following two work-outs will help you achieve this.

WORK-OUT 9: THINKING, FEELING AND BEHAVING

How you respond to situations depends on your previous experiences, your spontaneous behaviour patterns and your early childhood messages – how you were told to think, feel and behave when you were small. Some of these messages may have been positive and helpful like 'You're good at figures', but many others may have been unhelpful such as 'You'll never amount to anything' and have caused you long-term stress. It is time to get rid of these unhelpful messages, it's time to kick those creatures off your shoulder!

Whatever creatures are on your shoulder, overleaf are some positive ways of thinking. Try to internalize them, think about them and accept those that apply to you. You may have been subjected to a great deal of rubbish over your lifetime but that does not mean that you still have to carry it about with you!

The Be Perfect Person
You have a strong feeling of guilt; you are anxious about making a total mess of things. You sometimes experience feelings of worthlessness and depression.

You need to give yourself permission to appreciate the wonderful variety of different human attributes and values.

The Pleasing People Person
You have a fear of being misunderstood. You constantly consider other people's needs and fear being rude to them. You have an inner thought of 'Nobody lets me be myself'.

You need to give yourself permission to please yourself and let others please themselves. Be free to like or dislike people. Remember, when people reject you, you don't have to reject yourself.

The Hurry Up Person
You often have a major feeling of panic, not being able to think and fatigue. You may experience a constant feeling of lateness and always hurrying to try to fit in too many things. You sometimes have a sense of not belonging.

You need to give yourself some selfish time.

The Be Strong Person
You often fear being unappreciated and want to stay invulnerable to others. You are easily bored. You can't get close to people and have a sense of being unlovable.

You need to share your feelings and ask for help.

The Try Harder Person
You have a fear of failure and may think 'I could be the greatest if I could be bothered' or 'I'm not as good as I think I am'.

You need to give yourself permission to fail – and to succeed – so that you can get on with things and feel successful.

Self-assertion statements

Self-assertion statements help establish new beliefs about yourself, and counter old ones. To do this:
- ✓ First identify an area of your life in which you would like to be more assertive, eg speaking out in meetings.
- ✓ Write a self-assertion statement (see below for how).
- ✓ Read it out loud to yourself at least twice today.

Write positively, using 'I' statements and the present tense:
   'I speak out clearly and confidently at meetings' *not* 'Speaking out in meetings terrifies me.'
   'I respect myself for my opinions and values. I am keen to put forward my ideas to others' *not* 'No one will listen to my point of view; I am not valued in the organization.'

Write down below an area of your life in which you would like to be more assertive ....
....
Now write down a self-assertion statement ....

Read the statement out loud to yourself, visualizing real-life situations where you can put the theory into practice. Imagine the tone of voice you would use; think about how you would feel and how others might react.

Be assertive about your worth. Look after yourself, emotionally, physically and mentally. Take selfish time and enjoy it, treat yourself to small luxuries and rebuild your self-esteem.

> **TRAINER'S WARNING**
> *Remember, people can't mind read. Only you can tell them how you are feeling, so do it!*

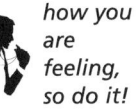

WORK-OUT 10: ASSERTIVENESS

In order to deal with stress you need to *address* the issues – you need to behave assertively. Remember, assertiveness is about being open, honest and direct. It is about being focused and asking for what you want or need, while recognizing that others also have needs. It is about recognizing that you and others have certain rights. Being assertive will help you to speak up, to deal with conflict and express your values and opinions. It will help you handle people, no matter their status. It will help you give and receive compliments, and criticism!

1 Expressing your feelings

To be assertive, you need to be able to express your feelings, even though other people may find them difficult to handle. Express your feelings and avoid turning them inward. In-turned anger can lead to depression. Say '*I* feel hurt when you treat me in that way' *not* '*You* make me feel hurt', as that gives your power away to the other person.

2 Giving and receiving compliments

You will get more out of life if you are able to give and receive compliments. Look for the good things in those around you, congratulate people rather than criticize them. Learn to enjoy, not shrink from, praise. It may sound simplistic, but to accept a compliment assertively all you really need to say is 'Thank you'. Beware of saying 'Thank you, *but*...', eg 'Thank you, but I really don't think I did that well.' Don't put yourself down. Assertiveness is about having the ability to respect and admit your own self-worth (receiving compliments), and that of other people (giving compliments). It is not about behaving in an embarrassed or humorous manner; it's about recognizing achievements without denial.

Now look at the following scenarios. Think first how you want to reply – that is your immediate response. Is your response assertive? If so, write it down below. If not, think about what you need to say to be assertive and write it down below.

A   Your colleague says 'You look good.' You say? ....
....

B A director says 'I heard that you did an excellent project and that it was accepted by the client, well done.' You say? ....
C Your boss says 'Congratulations, you are our lead salesperson again this month.' You say? ....
....
D A colleague has just secured a major contract with a firm you have been working on for months. What do you say? ....

3 Speaking in meetings
The following tips will help you speak up in meetings:
- ✓ Speak out early, even if it is only to say 'Good morning'. This will stop you thinking 'I'm the only one who hasn't spoken so far' and getting yourself into an anxious state.
- ✓ Keep contributions short to ensure that people keep listening and don't get bored.
- ✓ Avoid interrupting others and don't let others interrupt you. Say 'I would like to finish my point.'
- ✓ Say 'Please be brief', 'Make a statement' or 'What is the point you are making?' Avoid saying 'With respect' or 'Can I just say?' Say instead 'I wish to say' or 'I think/feel that...'
- ✓ Make at least one positive contribution, even if it is just agreeing, otherwise you may sit there thinking that everyone is involved and positive except yourself. This is *active* rather than passive agreement.
- ✓ Speaking up is easy if you believe that you are of worth. So realize that you are as OK as everyone else.
- ✓ Ask for clarification if anything seems unclear. It is also a sign that you are listening to the discussion.
- ✓ Avoid worrying about sounding stupid, and speak out if you really don't understand or agree with something.
- ✓ Check out whether other people agree or disagree with what is being said.

- ✓ Ask for feedback by asking the others at the meeting for their reaction to your ideas.
- ✓ Always confirm what people think they have to go away and do (their 'actions').

4 Saying No to a particular request

Saying No can be a stressful experience. The following tips will help you say No when you want to:

- ✓ Start by realizing that you are entitled to say No. With practice, you will learn to say No without feeling guilty.
- ✓ Recognize how to use language in a way that positively expresses what you really want. That means not saying Yes when you really mean No! It means not getting pulled down avenues you don't want to go, resulting in a labyrinth of irrelevant argument. You need to continue to make your point, 'No, I am unable to do that.' You can add 'sorry' if you think it appropriate but try to just say No.
- ✓ Demonstrate that you are hearing what the other person is saying. 'Yes, I do realize that you have personal problems at home, however, No, I cannot change the agreed arrangements.'
- ✓ Empathize with the other person about their situation, try to see the world through their eyes. However, if you really cannot help, say No again. For example, 'That sounds very difficult for you, and I understand your concerns. However, I cannot help on this occasion.'
- ✓ If you do feel able to respond to their position, you could offer a compromise. However, recognize your fallback position; how far you are prepared to alter your needs to accommodate the other person's wishes.

5 Establishing your values

People you like usually share your values (on politics, religion, race, gender and sexuality). You probably find it easier to get on with such people, and are likely to be assertive with them. Conversely, you tend to be less assertive with people you don't like. You may dislike them with good reason (maybe they hold racist or sexist views), but beware of not liking them for the wrong reasons – maybe you don't like their appearance or accent, maybe you resent their success. Be aware of why you like or dislike somebody, and your prejudices. Treat everyone fairly, regardless of their values (and in spite of your prejudices). Assert your own values in both your words and deeds. Speak honestly and directly, while recognizing that others also have values.

6 Rights of mind

How good are you at standing up for your rights? *You do have certain rights*. Lawyers may disagree with this wording, but for the purposes of this book consider your rights from a *moral* rather than a strict legal perspective.

The essence of assertiveness is recognizing that both you, and other people, have certain rights.

- ✓ You have the right to be heard, but equally you need to listen to others. You have the right to assert yourself, and so do other people.
- ✓ You have the right to state what you want, but you also need to recognize others' wants.
- ✓ You have the right to feel, but need to realize that other people have emotions too. Treat people as emotional human beings not as roles.
- ✓ You have the right to make mistakes. Remember that 'people who never make mistakes never make anything'.
- ✓ You have the right to be protected by the law, but you also need to live within the law.
- ✓ You have the right to free speech, but remember the effect your language will have upon others if you make racist, sexist or abusive comments.
- ✓ You have the right to feel secure, but remember that security is a state of mind and comes from within. Avoid creating insecurity by stirring up fear, anxiety and destructive gossip.

- ✓ You have the right to be happy, so if you were given a joyless script as a child then give yourself permission to change it. Try saying 'It's OK to be happy'.
- ✓ You have the right to be ill, so stop trying to play the martyr. Look after your physical and mental health.
- ✓ You have the right to be treated with respect, but remember, you also need to treat others with respect.
- ✓ You have the right to grieve, so give yourself permission to cry, feel sad and express you feelings.
- ✓ You have the right to give others their rights, so learn to empower people.
- ✓ You have the right to enjoy your sexuality, as long as it is not in the form of harassment or impinges upon other people's boundaries.
- ✓ You have the right not to be overlooked, but it is up to you to make your mark and be seen.
- ✓ You have the right not to be emotionally abused, however, people cannot read your mind so you need to tell them when you feel this way.
- ✓ You have the right not to be physically abused so it is up to you to distance yourself from the perpetrator. This is easier said than done for many people, but if you work on your own feelings of self-worth and self-love then you will reach a stage of recognizing that you are no longer prepared to live or to work where such behaviour exists.

About you checklist

- ✓ Use self-assertion statements to get rid of any negative 'creatures' on your shoulder.
- ✓ Remember, assertiveness is about being open, honest and direct. It is about recognizing your rights, wants and needs, and those of others.

Keeping Fit

Keeping Fit

Congratulations on finishing the book! Hopefully you have enjoyed the experience and gained from the advice and insights offered.

As you have discovered, stress management is a vital skill. But like any skill, practice makes perfect, and the more times you use it the better you get at it. You need to keep skills fit, and this is what the final part of this book is all about...

Keeping fit

As mentioned at the very start of this book, stress management is a key skill for success and happiness at both work and home – and it is important you don't let it slip.

You need to keep on your toes, keep practising. If you feel your skills slipping then look back through the book again, remind yourself of the key learning points, even run through a couple of exercises. Better still, set yourself some real-life targets now to keep yourself up to scratch. These could be anything from taking a daily walk to spoiling yourself with a visit to a health farm!

Make a note of your targets in your personal fitness plan below (bearing in mind the benefits it will bring you, or others). Specify actions and timescales; this will keep you focused and fit.

Personal fitness plan

Target/Action	By when?	✓
....		
....		
....		
....		
....		
....		
....		
....		
....		
....		
....		
....		
....		

Further Reading/ Bibliography

Further reading/bibliography

Civil, Jean, *Sexuality at Work*, Chrysalis Books, 1998

Davidson, Marilyn, and Cooper, Cary, *Stress and the Woman Manager*, Martin Robertson & Co, 1983

Ellis, A, 'The basic clinical theory of rational-emotive therapy', *Handbook of Rational-Emotive Therapy*, Springer Publishing Co, 1977

Ellis, A, *Humanistic Psychotherapy: The rational-emotive approach*, Julian Press, New York, 1973

Evans, Mark, *Instant Stretches for Stress Relief*, Lorenz Books, 1997

Hargreaves, Gerard, *Stress Management*, Marshall Publishing, London, 1998

Holmes, T H, and Rabe, R H, 'The Social Readjustment Rating Scale', *Journal of Psychosomatic Research*, Vol 2, No 2, 1967

Ishmael, Angela, with Alemoru, Bunmi, *Harassment, Bullying & Violence at Work*, Spiro Press, 1999

Priest, Simon, and Welch, Jim, *Creating a Stress-free Office*, Gower Publishing, 1998